Fight City Hall and Win! The Handbook

Roger Hedgecock
12/16/93

Roger Hedgecock
with Francine Phillips

Fight City Hall — and Win!

Copyright © 1993

By Roger Hedgecock
with Francine Phillips

Library of Congress Catalog Card Number: 93-61715
ISBN: 0-942259-09-2
Co-Edition by Westerfield Enterprises, Inc. and Write Now!

For information, contact
Write Now!
P.O. Box 3987
La Mesa, CA 91933-3987

Cover Design and Typesetting: The Art Ranch
Printing: Vanard Lithographers

Printed in the United States of America

There are many people to thank for help and cooperation in getting this book published. Thanks go to KSDO staff Gayle Falkenthal, the Executive Producer of my show, Marna McClure, Producer and Mark Carpowich, Intern for their help and support. A special thanks to my listener Mike Landry, who volunteered his time to compile statistics from the Registrar of Voters office and from the helpful staff of that office.

Finally, thanks to Francine Phillips for helping make this book a reality and to our long-suffering spouses, Mike Canrinus and Cindy Hedgecock for putting up with us until it was finished.

Table of Contents

Preface

I used to say I would never write a book. Everything I had to say, I said on my KSDO radio show from 12:20 to 3 p.m. Monday through Friday. If people listened to the show, there was no need for a book. And being the most listened-to talk show in San Diego history, I thought a book would be unnecessary.

I was sadly mistaken.

However long I talk with people on the air about the issues facing San Diego and the heroes trying to do something about them, it is simply impossible for most people to listen to every minute of my show. Particularly those with productive jobs.

But built into the dynamic of my Community Forum is the fact that sometimes just one call can change the whole character of an issue. Sometimes the right person gathers up the courage to call and truth goes over the airwaves, loudly and clearly, for all to hear. And then people respond to that truth and more truth comes out. That's the excitement of live talk.

I began to recognize that the occasional listener might find it difficult to keep up with the many themes and stories and on-going crusades that regular listeners hear developing on a daily basis.

My first book, written with Francine Phillips, was a primer, explaining the way San Diego is, how it got this way, what makes it work or not work, and who's done what to whom. The book, America's Finest City: If We Say It Enough We'll Believe It became the best-selling locally published book in the history of San Diego.

Still, this was not enough.

*People listening to my show continuously requested a newsletter to keep them current, to fill in the gaps in our stories and to find out how some of these stories concluded. I finally gave into this pressure and, again with the help of Francine Phillips, my monthly newsletter, **The Roger Report** was born and became the most widely-read local newsletter ever.*

And still this wasn't enough.

The remarkable stories of San Diegans and their efforts to make a better life, unfolded on my show with a regularity that demanded more than just the verbal attention that you pay to them within the talk show format. These people's lives were making a larger statement. A statement about the kind of America we could become again. A statement about the kind of community to which we could certainly aspire. The kind of people we could be — active, caring, involved, committed.

Within the pages of this book you will cheer, weep and grind your teeth, perhaps all three at once. But at the end you will be a different person — empowered, motivated and part of the solution.

Introduction

It's the oldest cliche in America - "You can't fight City Hall." The good news is, it's not true. In fact, this book will show you how to do just that. You will read the stories of brave people fighting for what's right. In the Appendix you will be armed with the names, addresses, phone and FAX numbers of elected and appointed officials at all levels of government. Now it's up to you to keep them accountable.

The bad news is this: Over the past 50 years, government has built huge bureaucracies that have promised to protect Americans from risk and harm. In programs ranging from apple subsidies to old age care, government has insinuated itself into almost every area of existence. All the while, trying to convince Americans to trade their traditional liberty for government guaranteed security.

Sadly, more and more Americans have experienced the dark side of this promise — the growth of massive bureaucracies. Dictatorial, insensitive, arrogant and ever-more powerful, these bureaucracies have developed on every level of government from City Hall to Congress. And the trade-off has become not liberty for security, but liberty for control. The result in our violent, crime-ridden society is loss of security, control and liberty.

Even worse, today's government seems biased against wealth accumulation, job production and individual initiative. Instead it is quickly creating vast constituencies of dependent Americans. A popular bumper sticker around San Diego sums up this frustrating situation this way — "Make Welfare as Hard to Get as Building Permits."

The key to a successful America is citizens who are informed. You may think you are relatively well-informed if you watch the nightly news, read all or part of the daily paper, and, of course, listen avidly to KSDO. Unfortunately, you're mistaken.

Only a very distorted and very narrow portion of the spectrum of knowledge is allowed to be made public. Bureaucrats and elected officials not only control information through the media, but are decreasing public access to information by secret votes, hidden agendas and unexplained changes. I know this is not what you were taught in your high school civics class. Today's real-life political process is an astounding contradiction to the picture of American government that most of us carry around in our head.

Let the Public Know

On my KSDO radio show, I try to bring out in the open how the news is manipulated and for whose benefit. For example, this year I told those who listen to my show that the budget of the San Diego City Planning Department four years ago was about $5 million and today it's about $10 million even though four years ago there were twice as many building permits to process. In other words, they have to work more slowly to get half the work done with twice the budget. You don't find out about this type of information from any other media source. It gets people's attention.

As more and more examples of this insanity get unearthed, I am determined to act on this type of information. Not just to have stomach-churning conversations about it, but to do something about it. Many of the local heroes in these pages started by engaging me and my KSDO listeners in a dialogue about some problem. Then they took action to solve it.

This book will demonstrate how the politics of today is out to get you and what you can do about it. However, don't mistake this book for a dry textbook on the theory of activism. In every chapter you will come to know citizens like yourself who decided that they were unhappy about something and that they were going to do something about it. Then they did it.

Everyday People

The people in this book did not start out as heroic figures, but their determination made them heroes.

Muriel Watson is the widow of a Border Patrol agent who was sick of the deception, rape, violence and murder taking place every night at the San Diego/Mexico border. Her concern was for the safety of both Mexican and American citizens. Her tactic was light. From this simple beginning, Light Up the Border became an effective mass movement that resulted in federal action at the international border. Muriel is not going to sit back ever again.

Cherie Chandler listened and listened with dismay to the growing demands made by liberal, activist sub-groups on her cherished country. She watched her country being compromised and become unrecognizable to her as her standards and beliefs were no longer *popular or in the majority. Silent No More burst forward when Cherie Chandler had had enough and now this group has an office, a strong membership and an agenda to get America back on track.*

Rob Miller is a young law student who was working himself through school with a job handling MediCal cases for the county. It was just a job. But soon the fraud and the waste and the departmental bias toward covering up fraud motivated him to act. He came forward on KSDO, blew the whistle and got fired, but he also fired up my listeners and caused far-reaching investigations and policy reviews to be implemented at all of the hospitals and at the state MediCal investigator's office. He didn't want to cause trouble and he certainly didn't want to lose his job. But he also knew right from wrong and had to speak out.

Sometimes, to protect your community, protect your business, or protect your family, you've simply got to step up and take a stand. In these pages, you will not only be inspired by others who have taken such a stand on an issue, you will be directed to the practical information you need to access and influence the decision-makers. And my KSDO Community Forum will be there, Monday through Friday from 12:20 to 3 p.m. on AM 1130, to coach you and give you access to like-minded listeners to help support your cause.

We want you to know you're not alone. We want you to know that there are others who have taken this step. We want you to know that not only have they taken this step, they have succeeded. They have "Fought City Hall" and won! You can too.

Chapter One

Addicted
To Bureaucracy

*The essence of Government is power;
and power, lodged as it must be in human hands,
will ever be liable to abuse.*
— James Madison, 1829

We, the people of the United States, have been victims of a 70 year-old habit that says, "When you have a good idea, make it a law and impose it on your fellow citizens." You can think of a thousand examples and so can I, from aircraft safety rules to zoning regulations.

This thrust to codify our idealistic goals and then implement them through a bureaucracy has in every case, sooner or later, resulted in the complete loss of the original idealism that drove the legislation in the first place. Absent idealism, the bureaucracy degenerates into corruption, fraud, waste and abuse. It is an inevitable process and it permeates every agency of every level of government. Now the cost of this bureaucratic habit is choking our economy, threatening our standard of living and also threatening an older American habit — living in freedom.

For example, in the early 20th century, the Progressive Movement sought to cure the "ills" of capitalism - railroad barons, filthy meat-packing houses, child labor sweatshops and more - with laws prohibiting these evils and inspectors to make sure they would never come back. Today the railroads are bankrupt and on the public dole. The meat-packing houses have more inspectors than meat-packers. The child labor laws have resulted in gangs of idle teenagers with little opportunity to get work when they need it. Laws and regulations have driven up prices and stifled opportunity.

How can anyone suggest that the original idealistic goals were not worthy? Certainly not I! But how can anyone today deny that their implementation has brought us the worst of both worlds?

The Customer's Always Right

Every one of us has come into contact with government employees doing their jobs. We've been to get our driver's license, perhaps a passport, to qualify for Social Security, to apply for veterans' benefits or a host of other government-run programs. The contrast between private sector and public sector service is noticeable to all. In not one place in government have I found even the common courtesy much less the efficiency that you would find going into a grocery store to pick up a carton of milk.

There is a very good reason for this, of course. The people who work for government are not acting irrationally at all. They are acting very rationally. You just need to understand that service to you is not their primary reason for being. You are not the "customer."

I happen to have a very cheerful mailman. But if I really have something important to communicate, I use a fax machine or the telephone. I do not use the U.S. Postal Service. If I have a very important package to send, I use the private sector alternatives, which are faster and cheaper.

I don't use the U.S. Postal Service, even though you and I subsidize the postal service to the tune of about $2 billion per year. As a government entity, the U.S. Postal Service is characterized by longer lines and more complicated regulations, resulting in more employees, resulting in more supervisors, resulting in higher prices. Resulting in poorer service to me.

The More You Have, The More You Have

In 1978, as a San Diego County Supervisor, I lead the charge to create a program that I called, "Workfare." Under Workfare, General Relief recipients who were able-bodied (most of them were) would be required to work in return for benefits. If they did not work or did not find work over a certain period of time, they would lose their benefits. Simple.

The biggest howl of protest came not from the welfare recipients, but from the welfare workers whose jobs were threatened. They were horrified by the notion that at some point in time there could be fewer people showing up to get welfare.

The entire incentive of the welfare department is to have more people on welfare, not less.

The entire incentive of the welfare department is to spend more time with those welfare recipients, not less. The entire incentive is not to disqualify people who are illegal aliens or who have hidden assets, or who have a spouse or boyfriend living at home or who have any of the other disqualifying factors. The incentive is to do nothing that would block applicants from getting the "free money." And if you try to change this incentive from within, like David Sossaman and Rob Miller tried — well, you can read their stories in Chapter Six.

The nature of the welfare bureaucracies is such that they will never stop growing. Their numbers will never decrease. This is not because these welfare and social workers are bad people. They simply know that their job security lies in signing up more people, not fewer.

And the more people who sign up for welfare means the more eligibility workers who may someday qualify to be a supervisor or get into middle management where they can do absolutely nothing. And get paid even more.

It's Everywhere

It's easy enough to criticize welfare. Let's look at law enforcement. Do you think that police officers actually want to automate their booking procedures to free themselves up for more time on patrol in the dangerous streets of our city? I guarantee you that's not true.

I guarantee you police officers will never want to spend less than an hour and a half on an arrest report back in their offices with a cup of coffee. Otherwise they would have to be out on your street figuring out why guys driving by in old cars are shooting at kids. These officers are not dumb. If the police could actually, at the scene of a burglary or other crime, enter a report into a comuputer in under ten minutes (and they can do that today with existing technology if they want to) then they would be out there on the streets nearly all the time. That would mean being at risk, being in danger - all the time!

Judges, who golf on Thursdays and insist that they work a full week, never want to come in at night or on the weekends. They never want to give their "clientele" a better service because then they might actually clean up the backlogged calendar and then what would happen to the increase in judges?

This same bureaucracy of the criminal justice system - from the beat cops to the judges' bench - rejoiced over the illegal 1/2 cent sales tax that was charged to San Diego County taxpayers. Dick Rider successfully sued to have your money returned to you (see Chapter 11) but it required more legislation to force the bureaucrats to finally give you your money back.

Contrast these welfare and police bureaucratic practices with the service you get from any private store. For example, look at the Sears Auto Service Departments. They have had their problems with shoddy practices and are bounding back with a new program of expanded hours, guaranteed time for specific repairs and an attitude that believes that only by increasing quality and lowering prices can they stay in business. Why don't we taxpayers demand the same attitude from our government services? When was the last time you heard of a government advertising a better service at a lower price to you, the taxpayer?

In Chapter Four you will read about Muriel Watson and her tremendous effort to impact illegal immigration. But does the Border Patrol really want to stop illegal immigration? If so, why wasn't it the Border Patrol who found the surplus steel runway plates in the National Guard Armory in Texas. It was Congressman Duncan Hunter's office that found them to build a border fence with National Guard welders.

Why was it that all those portable lights that the Border Patrol already had in their inventory did not shine until Muriel Watson demanded lights on the border?

Do you think it's possible that the Border Patrol will not do more than the minimum required, and only that because of their individual dedication? Would they use the statistics of illegal immigration to support their jobs before actually going out, doing the job and just maybe working themselves out of a job? Do you think they fear working themselves out of a job more than they fear your backlash against them for not doing the job they were sent there to do?

These are questions that have never been answered and no politicians, however tough, have ever asked them.

A Drought In The Budget

Here's another example. A few years ago when we had a drought, the government said, "Save water, there's a drought. You all need to change your shower heads, stop watering your lawn, washing your car or hosing down your sidewalks" So everybody did. As soon as there was a lower flow of water, the bureaucrats at the water authority realized that if people used less water, they'd be paying less money. If they paid less money, then the spending budget of the water authority would not be met.

So, the first thing they did was raise the price of water. A confused public reacted, Wait a minute! You mean the reward for cutting back on the use of water is that we pay more? Where are you guys coming from?The public forgot how bureaucracies are set up. The bureaucracy was acting absolutely logically in its context - in its own best interest. The water districts had a certain number of goals for capital improvements, a certain number of staff, a certain way of doing things, cars to take home and conferences to attend in Washington D.C. and Sacramento. This is what they had to do. They couldn't fire anybody. They certainly were not going to cut necessary programs. The public would just have to pay more.

They never thought, like the corner grocer, If I lose customers, I've got to cut prices and increase volume in order to make money. People say, "Why can't we run government like a business?" Well, the awful truth is government is set up to run exactly the opposite of business.

The fact is, these bureaucracies have exactly the opposite incentive of your local food store. Say your local store would like more customers. The way they get more customers is by having better quality food at a lower price than the guy down the street. It is just the opposite in every single bureaucracy, where service to the client is not necessarily linked to job security for the people doing that work. The slower government moves, the more complicated and less understandable its rules, the more government workers will be needed.

What's The Incentive?

We need to realize that the evil of bureaucracy is not the fault of the people who work within it. The nature of bureaucracy is the fault of the people who design the incentives for it.

Say each member of Congress was given $1 million cash, tax-free, for every year the federal budget was balanced, how many years

8

do you think it would take to get the budget balanced? ONE, of course. This would only cost taxpayers $435 million per year. Right now we are wasting $1 billion a day in federal deficit spending. A billion dollars that we don't have is being spent each day by the federal government because the incentives are backwards.Here's how Congress really works. The more the Congressmembers give away your money and your grandchildren's money to placate insistent voices of high-powered lobbyists, the more chance they have of receiving campaign donations from those groups for re-election. The incentives produce the result.

If we want lower federal deficits, more responsive congressmembers and a lower influence from pleading lobbyists and pressure groups, we've got to turn the incentives around. If we want fewer welfare clients, fewer welfare workers and more people productively employed, then we've got to turn the incentives around.

If we want more effective law enforcement, we've got to turn the incentive around and reward the officer on the beat, who is the lowest paid cop in the department. All he wants is to get one step above that as sergeant or lieutenant so he will never again have to face the stream of nasty, violent criminals that are loose on America's streets. Why not pay the cop on the beat the most money, and decrease the salary for the paper-pushers? Our incentives are all wrong.

Why do the teachers in schools make the least amount of money? (In many school districts less than the people who sweep up after the school day is done.) Why do we accept that and expect the teachers to turn out quality graduates?

You'll read in Chapter Seven about Katie Zolezzi who wanted to run a day care facility centered on the arts. She wanted to take care of children who would otherwise be latchkey kids.

This tremendous need has been brought up again and again in the public mind by articles, books and television news. In fact, so great is the concern that the city council passed a special ordinance commanding its bureaucracy to give special treatment - favorable treatment - to those who come in with applications for day care centers.

But there was no incentive given to carry out the wishes of the council. So you will read about the bureaucratic nightmare Katie Zolezzi has had to go through and is still fighting. And when you read about her torture, you'll wonder what "unfavorable treatment" would be!

Once we look at the incentives for bureaucracies we can understand what we have gotten into in this country - lower quality services, higher and higher taxes, more and more onerous regulations throttling the life-blood of our economy. We bought it. We paid for it. It is working the way it was designed to work. If it was designed differently, it would work differently.

You can't protest the lack of cops on the beat without understanding why they're not there. There are plenty of cops. You can't protest overburdened welfare without understanding that we built a system designed to become overburdened. You can't complain about illegal aliens coming to this country before you realize that the system of incentives of the Border Patrol are designed to allow the border to remain "open."

Once you understand the nature of the bureaucracy, then you can begin to see how to turn it around. Once we demand that teachers be the highest paid, that the cops on the beat be the highest paid and once we remove the incentive to avoid risk and work, government will change.

Let's put the incentive back into these jobs to do more, not only with pay but with increased authority. Put the teachers back in charge of the classroom and pay them more for positive results. Get the cop back out on the street and give them bonuses for arrests leading to convictions. It's a matter of realizing what has gone wrong and turning it around.

There Oughta Be A Law!

The next time somebody comes along with a good idea and wants to pass a law to go with it — let's say health care at the federal level — put the consumers in charge. That's the way it works in the private sector. The consumer's choice of where to spend money is the critical factor that guarantees the efficiency and quality found the entire private sector economy. That's why advertising is there, that's why marketing is there, that's why packaging is there - to get you to choose their product. Producers are in competition and competition results in a higher quality product at a lower price.

If health care is the problem (not health insurance, but health care) then the best plan is the one that puts responsibility for the choice and the payment in the hands of the ultimate consumer - the patient. If the patient has the choice of what to do and when to do it, along with responsibility to pay for it, or to pay for the insurance for it, or to pay for some part of the insurance for it, there is responsibility along with choice and you will have an excellent health care plan.

But if, like the Clinton plan, you start with big government and trickle down you are going to have layers and layers of bureaucrats insensitive to your needs and running a multi-billion dollar more-than-it-should-cost program to deliver mediocre care to people when they get around to it. If you think this is an exaggeration, just ask the people who use the Veterans Administration Hospital.

Reinvent Bureaucracy

Reinventing government is a great phrase. In the Clinton administration, unfortunately, it means shuffling the bureaucratic titles and leaving the incentive system in place. After 70 years of this process, we are dangerously close to a bureaucratic dictatorship in this country. Elected officials come and go, but the bureaucrats who run those elected officials stay.

During the course of their careers, bureaucrats may go through five or six presidents, a dozen governors at the state level or a host of mayors and city council members at the local level. But their policies, inclinations and incentives remain. No matter how many times the

San Diego City Council passes an ordinance for day care centers, if the planning department process and regulatory incentives are against development and construction of new businesses, they will not differentiate when it comes to day care centers. They will be obstructionist to all.

We've got to rethink each one of these cases and put the taxpayer, the consumer, in charge to restrict the power of the un-elected bureaucrats.

Ironically, their power has now been increased by term limits. Term limits will get rid of career politicians and force the politicians in office to be more responsive. But term limits will not stop the growing bureaucratic tyranny that goes on in every administration at every level of government.

Last year our Congress got involved when consumers were outraged at the price of cable television. Basic service costs too much, they said, and Congress agreed. So Congress held its hearings and did its investigations and passed the Cable Act of 1993 that was supposed to lower everybody's cable bill.

Except, of course, lots of peoples' bills went up. Cable companies simply changed their billing so that the basic service rates went down, but extra charges were added for other services. Congress was duped by a regulated industry that has no competition, no consumer choice, and, therefore, no incentive to lower the prices and raise the quality. This is the same Congress that is going to give you better health care. Right!

Ultimately, it is up to you and me to challenge our politicians and bust the bureaucracies. Americans are just now re-awakening to the fact that elected officials work for them. The hard part will be getting elected officials to do the same with the bureaucrats. All the staff recommendations, hidden budget items, regulatory roadblocks, volumes of paper work, let alone the crippling fees, have to be called into question and brought back under control. The only way to make your elected officials hold the bureaucrats accountable to them is to make elected officials accountable to you.

Chapter Two

Do You See
What I See?

*Every time we turn our heads the other way
when we see the law flouted—
when we tolerate what we know to be wrong—
when we close our eyes and ears to the corrupt
because we are too busy, or too frightened—
when we fail to speak up and speak out—
we strike a blow against freedom and decency and justice.*
—Robert F. Kennedy, 1961

You don't hear the term "moral outrage" much anymore. We hear plenty about "black rage" or "teen angst" and now "Mexican Dignity," and other descriptions of subgroups that have risen up in anger against supposed injustice. But the concept of becoming outraged over a moral issue is pretty passe. Taking a stand for morality could put you on unpopular ground.

But the story you are about to read is one of such total moral depravity that if you are not outraged by it (although many politicians and officials are not) you may want to take a moral inventory of what you believe is right and good and where you draw the line. I draw the line here.

I See It But I Don't See What I'm Seeing

Bill Brown is a bicyclist who always enjoyed the wide expanse of Balboa Park. He pedaled regularly through its winding pathways, shaded with magnificent trees and surrounded with green lawns, rose gardens, children with balloons, clever mimes and ice cream stands. One sunny Saturday, he was cycling by Marston Point in Balboa Park when he stopped for a rest. He watched as a shiny, late-model car pulled up to the side of the curb. It was driven by a successful-looking white, executive-type man. Bill shaded his eyes from the sun watched as a young boy, 12 or 13 years old, emerged from the nearby bushes, went up to the window, spoke to the man and got in the car.

The car drove off and just as Bill was about to go, another car came along. Curiously, the same thing occurred. A boy got into the car and the car drove off. Something was going on. A third car came along, another boy ran out of the bushes. Then the first, original car pulled up again and the boy jumped out and ran off.

Suddenly, Bill understood what he was seeing. It had taken a while. But what he was seeing were middle-class men buying sex from young boys in broad daylight in the middle of Balboa Park. Once he saw what he was seeing, he looked more closely. These prostitutes were not only young boys, they were illegals and mostly drug abusers.

What Bill was seeing was the very worst possible central knot in a tangled web of social ills. What he was seeing was illegal immigration, child abuse, homosexuality, prostitution and drug abuse being bought and paid for by middle-class San Diegans.

"I was outraged," said Bill when he called my KSDO show to talk about what he had seen. "I was so incensed that when the next car pulled up, I went to the driver's window and said, `What are you doing?'"

"The driver said, `It's none of your business.' But I decided to make it my business, so I took down his license plate number. I'm going to go back again on Saturday and I want to invite your listeners to come with me."

"Great," I said. "We'll get your number off the air for people to call in and contact you. Call me back next week and let me know what happens."

So What?

The more I thought about that call, the more disturbed I got. Here we are in what we like to call America's Finest City and yet we have this terrible child abuse taking place in broad daylight.

I'm going to stop this abuse, I thought. I'm going to let everyone know about this situation in the Balboa Park and certainly, by sheer embarrassment, the politicians and the police and the Border Patrol will do something about it.

When Bill called back the next week, he sounded discouraged. Only a few people had been interested in joining his efforts. When they showed up at Marston Point, the Mexican kids yelled at them, threw rocks, and told them to leave. The johns driving the cars were not deterred by those taking down their license plate numbers. No one seemed to care. He said he was going to be transferred with his job out of San Diego and it all seemed hopeless.

I told him to contact the City Council and the Balboa Park committee, the police and the Border Patrol and call me back. Meanwhile, more listeners were solicited to help.

And some of them did care. One listener, Jim Tapscott, had heard the very first plea for help on his car radio when he was driving to pick up his wife. He took a detour to Marston Point on his own. There he saw just what Bill had talked about — men buying sex with young Mexican boys. The children are brought up from Mexico, sold for sex, encouraged to take drugs to ease the pain of their existence, and then forced to continue their prostitution to support their drug habit. It amounts to child slavery openly trafficking in our city.

"It was something that I just could not drive away from and forget about," said Jim. "I was determined to make a commitment to bring an end to this activity."

So the fledgling group began to hold meetings and my KSDO student intern, Rachael Laffer, went to the park to help in their efforts and assist them in getting organized. They continued to take down license numbers. Their efforts brought them attention from San Diego Youth and Community Services.

You Can't Solve This Problem

But the SDYCS was less than supportive. We know all about this problem, they said. It's been going on for at least the last eight years. Two years ago this issue made national news with Dan Rather and CBS News. We can't stop it. Our approach is to give these kids food and condoms to make it tolerable. This is survival sex. They have no other choice. You are driving them to other parts of the city where we can't watch them.

"It seemed as if they were afraid for us to intervene," said Tapscott, "as if we would interfere with their program, or threaten their funding. Somehow they had more interest in working with the problem than simply putting an end to it."

Meanwhile, gay community activists refused to accept responsiblity for the problem. Only a small percentage of gays are pedophiles, they insisted, less than 30 percent. But at the same time, at the Gay Pride Parade, as they marched past Marston Point they laughingly called it the Fruit Loop. The Uptown Examiner editorialized on the subject and insisted that it was consensual sex and concluded that it was a private matter.

So, Bill Brown moved away and Jim Tapscott took over the group, still determined to bring the public face to face with this issue. His group started taking video cameras to Marston Point, hoping to get some television news coverage that would shame the participants away from Marston Point.

And they did get television coverage. Only it came in the form of criticism from KGTV Channel 10's Stephen Clark. He called them "video vigilantes" and criticized their concern. It was a typical liberal media, politically correct distortion of the truth thatfailed to look at this pedophilia and prostitution and say, This is Wrong.

I really went crazy about this on my show. Because, in my mind, this is a slam-dunk issue. The liberal media wants us to wink and tolerate children being sold for sex in Balboa Park and denounces efforts to stop it. This is a watershed moral issue. Forget saving the Starlight Theater, worrying about the size of the Municipal Gym or bringing Pandas in from China. We don't even have to have a discussion about a campground that would provide shelter and protection to homeless families.

Because the fact is, our Balboa Park is now internationally known as a place for pedophiles to buy helpless, drugged and hungry children for their own sexual satisfaction. And so far this community allows it.

Call The Cops

What about the police? That's another issue. For a while there were increased patrols and the activity subsided a little. But that was a temporary respite. The police consider it a problem for the Border Patrol. They are not allowed to detain illegal aliens anyway, unless they are actually caught in the act of a crime.

The Border Patrol, on the other hand, is stretched enough along the border. Because of the public concern, they did increase a presence at Marston Point, but it is really an exercise in futility. In the first place, the Border Patrol is not allowed to pursue anyone on the freeway. So, when they come along in their jeeps, the kids all run through a hole in the fence and race onto the free median. It becomes a stand-off until the Border Patrol goes away.

When, in the rare case, the Border Patrol does apprehend these kids for prostitution or drug charges, they are taken to the Mexican consulate in San Diego. From there, the kids are simply taken to the other side of the border and let go. There is no detention, no child protective services, no agency in Mexico committed to dealing with this problem. These are "throwaway" kids who have been mostly sexually abused and are running away or have been kicked out of their homes in Mexico. They have no where to go, no where to live, no where to turn.

Out of this frustration and bureaucratic maze, Jim called my show. He seemed to be the end of his rope. Jim recalls what happened next:

"I called the community forum on KSDO and talked to Roger one more time and he just let me talk. All of my emotions came tumbling out and I expressed my agony over these pathetic children and the coldness of the bureaucracy and the self-protectiveness of the social agencies involved. It was all too much for me. `Where is the church?' I asked, `Where are the people who believe that this is immoral? How can we allow this to go on?' That day the deadlock broke."

That day San Diego City Councilwoman Judy McCarty called Jim and asked for a tour of Marston Point to check it out. She saw what was going on and drafted a city policy that would call for the police to impound the cars of johns soliciting for sex. On the first round, this was voted down, but she is working on another car impound approach that might be adopted by the City Council.

Meanwhile, Jim's group contacted more agencies and churches and started to get some response. Then they chose a name - PARK - People's Actions for Rescuing Kids. And beginning last October there were 200-300 volunteers collecting food and clothing to give to the kids. On Friday nights, Spanish-speaking volunteers go down and spend time with the kids. Some are totally tough and derisive. But some are opening up. These are kids, from ages 12 to 20, who have never had anyone care about them before.

"I know that what we are doing is right," said Jim Tapscott. "We've had support from the beat cops who know the real problems. The only flak we've had is from the bureaucrats and the administrators who say that this is a problem that cannot be solved. They say this is a problem that will never end. As long as there is a demand, they say, there will be a supply.

"But I think that we can work on that too. These people who buy sex from children need help too. Coming down and breaking their windshields will not help. We just have to work our way through all of it. Maybe, because of what we are doing, somebody will turn to someone they think is doing this and say, `Hey, how about getting some help for your problem?' Maybe that's the way this will end."

It will not end until we make it end. This issue is going to be ignored by the politicians, downplayed by the police and abandoned by the Border Patrol unless we who are morally outraged come forward and say, "Enough! This has to be stopped!" Jim Tapscott and his group of volunteers have made a start. They are heroes.

Today's Low Moral Fiber Diet

The world is not what we think it is. The moral convictions that many of us take for granted are not necessarily shared by those politicians, bureaucrats and officials who are in power. Our outrage is not shared. Amazing at it may seem to us they will only care when we make them care. Our only power in this situation is our power to be heard, loud and clear, without ceasing, until it is simply more inconvenient to allow this to continue than to work out a way to put an end to it.

Volunteers are still needed in this battle. You can become involved by writing to PARK Committee, 8062 Clairemont Mesa

Blvd., Suite 3, San Diego, CA 92111. The swell is rising and is going to become a tidal wave of concern until it's accomplished.

This one we must win.

Chapter Three

Make
Yourself Heard

The feeling of the nation must be quickened;
the conscience of the nation must be roused;
the propriety of the nation must be startled;
the hypocrisy of the nation must be exposed;
and its crimes against God and man
must be proclaimed and denounced.
—Frederick Douglass, 1852

Have you ever wondered how people get in the news? How the news media selects who is heard, who is quoted, who is seen?

This mystery is not so mysterious at all, especially in San Diego. Here, the television and radio news folks generally believe that anything written in the Union-Tribune is news. Anything that does not get play in the U/T is not news. Consequently, if you and your group want community-wide awareness of an event or opinion or activity, the easiest way to achieve that is to be included in the Union-Tribune.

Now, you ask yourself, how do I do that? This is also not a mystery. Reporters, just like every other human being, are constantly seeking to make their jobs easier. When you call with an exciting story, they're going to be inclined to listen to what you have to say. What are they listening for? Here's an example of what catches a reporter's attention:

A protest is coming up Thursday at noon at City Hall about gays in the military. Organized by Silent No More. Over 200 people are expected to participate.

Contact: Name and phone.

That kind of information, whether phoned in or faxed in or put in a press release does get listened to and does form the basis of what gets subsequently known as "news." Now, of course, it is up to you to hold it on the right day, in the right place and to get those 200 people really there. Credibility will make or break you and you usually only have one shot at it.

Get It In Writing

If you have a protest, a rally, an initiative petition, or a hearing coming up on a matter that calls for a wider community understanding of your point of view, the traditional avenue is the press release — a one-page summary of your position including Who, What, Where, When and Why. This can guide the reporter to your point of view and to make the reporter's job as easy as possible.

A press release should be readable and straightforward without any superlatives. If it is well-written, typed and double-spaced it will have a better chance of being used, since many papers now have scanners and choose the releases that can be scanned directly into the database. If you had to choose between 300 releases for a four-inch space, which would you choose?

Location, Location, Location

When you are staging a rally, protest or event, don't forget that the location is as important to the television media as the idea. When we staged our tax protest last April 15, we held it on the very lawn of the Midway Post Office, where hundreds of cars were lined up to kiss their hard-earned tax dollars goodbye. It was natural to combine the already newsworthy story of the tax deadline with our protest against paying them and it made it a heck of a lot easier for the television cameras to make just one stop for both stories.

On the other hand, if you want to get in-depth coverage from the print media, hold your meeting near the reporter's office. Many community newspapers would appreciate this courtesy and will give you much more coverage and visibility than one inch in the Union-Tribune.

KSDO - Ahead Of The Headlines

In many cases in San Diego, a single phone call to my KSDO talk show has accomplished the same result as an item in the Union Tribune. I have nearly the same number of listeners per week as the U/T has subscribers.

Muriel Watson and Dave Sossaman could have faxed themselves silly trying to convince reporters that what they were doing was important. Once they discussed it on my show and once there was a public groundswell of concern, then it became newsworthy. The newspaper found itself in the position of following what we had established on the radio show.

In the case of the Rob Miller MediCal fraud, Rob was on our show reporting his story of fraud. The next day he was fired. Several weeks later the U/T did an outstanding five-part series on the topic of MediCal fraud, although not from an employee standpoint and Rob Miller was not mentioned at all. But the issue became "news" and that's what counts.

Who You Gonna Call?

In the appendix under "Media" you will find the phone and fax numbers of several Union-Tribune reporters, community newspapers, television and radio news outlets. Media in San Diego works like a revolving door with many of the same writers, reporters and newscasters going in and out of the various news outlets. So if you really want to be accurate, it would be best to invest in a directory like the Finder Binder, which includes all media and is updated quarterly. Otherwise, send your news to the "Assignment Editor" at a television station, the "News Editor" and "City Editor" at a newspaper and the "News Director" at a radio station. When in doubt, call the receptionist or news clerk to find out who is best suited for your pitch.

Hear Me Roar

Whatever your strategy for getting heard, understand that news coverage does make a difference. When the City Council quietly proposed to inflict a $5.00 parking fee on the beaches and Balboa Park, they weren't expecting the public to get involved. In fact, they had already asked City Manager Jack McGrory to get bids on building the kiosks and putting in the meters. But when this little proposal became known, all hell broke loose.

We talked about it on KSDO and it became BIG news. State Assemblyman Mike Gotch embarrassed himself by publicly suggesting that the city council should just add a new utilities tax to everybody's bill instead of the parking fee!. That got everyone's attention.

Then the Zoo jumped in and said that they couldn't keep their lot free if the other lots in the Balboa Park were charging, so they announced a $5 parking fee as well. That got the attention of the Convention and Visitor's Bureau. We devoted an entire KSDO remote broadcast in Pacific Beach to this issue, where a listener announced that a referendum petition was already underway. That got the politicians' attention.

The City Council realized that they had to take a second look at this idea. Four public hearings were scheduled.

The public was heard at the hearings. Over 2,000 people attended the hearings to protest the fees. This was news. And the 200 that packed the City Council chambers with signs, particularly one that said, simply, "Fire McGrory" — they were news. That night the City Council, in an 8 to 1 vote (with George Stevens dissenting) agreed to drop the fee proposal. Mayor Golding who had voted originally for the parking fee said that this notion would never again be brought up as long as she was in office.

That, finally, was good news.

Chapter Four

Let There Be Light

*Publicity is justly commended as
a remedy for social and industrial diseases.
Sunlight is said to be the best of disinfectants;
electric light the most efficient policeman.*
—Louis D. Brandeis, 1913

In 1988, Dairy Mart Road, next to the international border, was not a safe place to be. It was like a DMZ - a twilight war zone. There was no fence across the border near Dairy Mart Road and every evening groups of immigrants would mass by the hundreds on a little hill across the border. Come sundown, they waded across the Tijuana River in the pitch dark, carrying meager bundles of belongings, trying to lift small children out of the mud, desperate to not get separated. All the while, the crossfire of "Coyotes," drug traffickers and Border Patrol agents rang out at close range. Thieves flashed knives and babies cried in the night. Every night.

Muriel Watson is the widow of a Border Patrol agent. The situation of illegal immigration was the topic of conversation among many groups, incuding Stamp Out Crime and the Crime Commission. Muriel attended as an interested citizen and many times as a member of a discussion panel. For years this talk and discussion routine prevailed and nothing happened to change anything. Yes, everyone agreed that the border was a disaster. But no one, in authority or not, wanted to act. We all turned our eyes away. Finally, in 1988 Muriel, out of her own simple frustration, decided to act.

Her timing could not have been worse. In 1985, illegal immigration had received national attention. In the legislature, Senator Alan Simpson of Wyoming and Congressman Romano Mazzoli from Kentucky drafted a bill to address the issue. The bill went through all the intricate and incredibly difficult committee processes and eventually became law. The 1986 Immigration Reform and Control Act

(IRCA) called for a fresh start. The Act granted amnesty to illegals, but ICRA also called for employor sanctions and stiffer border controls.

Illegal immigration fell that first year from 60 to 70 percent. The Mexicans felt that we might actually be serious about this issue. But the Reagan administration only half-heartedly supported the effort because it wanted lots of cheap labor to weaken American labor unions and support agribusiness. Reagan had absolutely no interest in controlling illegal immigration and neither did Bush. Until the passage of NAFTA in 1993 seemed threatened by the renewed flood of illegal immigration, Clinton didn't care either.

Consequently, the IRCA was a failure. Within two years, apprehensions of illegals had climbed and within four years, by 1990, they were nearly back to where they were bfore IRCA.

But the legislators were still congratulating themselves, patting themselves on the back and telling America that the problem of illegal immigration was solved. Muriel Watson stood up to tell them that it was not solved and her message was absolutely not welcome.

Muriel's message was simply this: Light Up the Border. The nightly crossings were dark and dangerous, not only for Americans on patrol, but for immigrants making the journey. The governments of both countries were winking at the problems. All Muriel wanted to do was shed some light.

As it turned out, Dairy Mart Road was in the City of San Diego and under the authority of the San Diego Police. Muriel found out that parking along the side of the road was legal. So she called her friends and neighbors and on Nov. 4, 1990, 23 automobiles parked their cars and shined their headlights into the pitch dark of the border no man's land.

A month later, on Dec. 2, she had 60 cars at the border. In January there were 150 cars.

After each event, Muriel would call me at KSDO. The first time she said, "Roger, I'm going down there! I'm going to park my car and put on my headlights to shine some light on the problem."

"Great!" I said. "Go for it, Muriel!"

The she called again.

"I'm going down to the border again, Roger," she said, "and this time fifteen of us are going."

"Good job!" I said. "Way to go!"

The next month she called again.

"It's working, Roger," she said. "We're going again."

Now I was inspired. If a group of Republican women could get out and demonstrate in a physically intimidating and dangerous setting, this was extraordinary. I called her up live in the middle of my radio show to find out more about it.

"I'm going too, Muriel," I finally said. "Give me directions." I invited my listeners to join us.

That night fifteen hundred people participated in the silent vigil that shed light on an issue that no one wanted to see. The Americans were from all races and cultures, from yuppies to seniors, all with their own reason to be there. Light Up the Border became a movement.

Singlehandedly, Muriel Watson took the uneasiness about the border situation, the generalized concern, the talk and the politics and focused everyone's attention on one thing that could make a terrible situation more tolerable. Light. And with that light reflecting on the hundreds of faces each night came the unmistakeable reality that the border was still out of control.

The Whole World Hears

The actions of this housewife have changed the international debate on our border issues. Even political foes like Senator Barbara Boxer and Governor Pete Wilson agree now that action must be taken. This kind of coalition would have been unthinkable a couple of years ago.

Finally, of course, Muriel did get her lights. In October, 1992, the Army Corps of Engineers installed a steel fence and permanent lights on an 11-mile stretch of border south of the Tijuana River. But Light Up the Border enlightened the entire world to the problem of illegal immigration.

Because of Muriel, the first-ever study of the cost of illegal immigration was completed. The tidalwave of immigration was estimated to cost local county and state agencies $146 million each year in San Diego County alone, and $3 1/2 billion in the state of California. These are net costs, taking into account the sales tax and other contributions that illegals are making. But the strain on the social services, the criminal justice system and the educational systems are being acknowledged at the same time our economy is in recession and our budget deficit is increasing. These costs have caused a backlash of emotion and concern.

NAFTA - Do We Hafta?

At the same time, there has been a riptide of opposition to NAFTA. By 1993, the North American Free Trade Agreement was just getting into the consciousness of most Americans and people began to wonder why illegal immigration was not being addressed. The promise of NAFTA is to open the border and the ordinary citizen is starting to say, "Hey, wait a minute!" So the cross current of concern for the border and concern about NAFTA has caused a confluence of opposition.

Consequently, it was no coincidence that Attorney General Janet Reno staged Operation Blockade at El Paso, Texas in Ross Perot's backyard. She took a relatively manageable border site to demonstate that the Clinton administration can solve the immigration problems and will solve them if we support NAFTA in return. Without Texas support, NAFTA is dead.

And if it takes Operation Blockade in San Diego or funding for a sewage treatment plant in the Tijuana River Valley to get our legislator's vote for NAFTA, well, thank you very much, we'll take them. And if San Diego County can send the President a monthly bill for services to illegal aliens that actually puts money back into our coffers, we'll take that too. And who started all of this? Muriel Watson.

When she began, Muriel Watson was a hard-working, honest, common sense American housewife. By 1992 she was a candidate. Muriel ran for the state senate and received 47,000 votes on the border issue alone. In 1993 she ran again. Muriel's not afraid of the system anymore. She is not frustrated (much) anymore because she knows that the system can work if you fight to make it work. She knows that she can fight — and win.

Chapter Five

What Can One Person Do?

*I have come to the conclusion
that one useless man is called a disgrace,
that two are called a law firm and
that three or more become a congress.*
—Peter Stone, "1776, A Musical Play"

The key ingredient in the success of the United States and the characteristic that sets us apart from all other human societies is our reliance on the individual. Our history can literally be told by telling the stories of determined individuals. The effect of a persistent individual is particularly important in San Diego, where without individual effort and leadership, nothing would ever get done at all. But you've read all about that in my first book, If We Say It Enough We'll Believe It.

I was reminded the other day of the impact of Ellen Wilson, wife of President Woodrow Wilson. She came to the District of Columbia from Georgia where she had been used to lots of beauty in her upper-class girlhood. She found Washington, D.C. to be somewhat stark.

During her term as First Lady there was a tremendous amount of discussion with Japan in the arms control debate, trying to avert World War I. As a consequence, the Wilsons and the Japanese Ambassador were fairly close friends. Mrs. Wilson, curious about the differences between Japanese and American culture, began to relate to the Ambassador's wife on the issue of beauty. She found that the Japanese think of themselves as the master appreciators of beauty. (Of course, that is all baloney. I've been to some of their cities and there is very little beauty. There's about three square inches of grass in all of Osaka. So, there is no beauty, but there is a cultural appreciation of beauty in the abstract.)

Anyway, out of that relationship between women came the first Cherry trees, given to the United States by the Japanese Ambassador and planted by the President and his wife around the reflecting pool. The display of cherry blossoms each Spring is now a national treasure called the Cherry Blossom Festival which ear year is appreciated by thousands of tourists.

That's the way things start. Someone decides that beauty is a big part of who we are and that if we can enhance our lives with it we should. All our anti-litter campaigns, anti-graffiti campaigns and tree-planting campaigns arise from determined individuals living out this belief.

The Greening Of San Diego

The Jacarandas for San Diego effort by Sylvia Simpson Coleman compares directly to the efforts of Ellen Wilson and to those of another woman in San Diego history who worked tirelessly to beautify our county — Kate Sessions. Sessions was a woman who, after the turn of the century, took up the crusade of transforming the near-barren land in the hillside above downtown into what is now Balboa Park. At the time, there was nothing there but chaparral. It looked then the way Tecolote Canyon looks today.

On National Arbor Day, 1908, Kate Sessions gathered together the city fathers. They were looking forward to the Panama-California Exposition in 1915. Kate Sessions pointed out that people were coming from all over the world. Where they had trees.

Sessions was aided and abetted by the Santa Fe railroad, which had brought from Australia a promising tree called the Eucalyptus.

They hoped to cut the trees into railroad ties. The railroad had searched the world for this tree and had grown acres of them in Rancho Santa Fe. In fact, they bought Rancho Santa Fe for pennies just for that purpose.

Well, Eucalyptus were, of course, completely unsuitable for rails. They split and twisted. So, Kate Session got them to plant trees in Balboa Park instead.

Sylvia Simpson Coleman was the direct descendent of this impulse to make our San Diego desert bloom in a significant way. Her dream was that San Diego could have a special identity in beauty. Coleman's hope was to make the annual blooming of the Jacarandas a county-wide festival, like Washington D.C.'s cherry blossoms, for the few weeks that the trees are in their purple glory. She envisioned the trees being planted in a continuous corridor along the freeway all the way to Tijuana.

First Sylvia started very small, with her garden club in La Jolla, but she had a very ambitious dream, very much like Kate Sessions had about Balboa Park.

Looking through the Sunday paper one day last year, my wife noticed a tiny item about Sylvia and the Jacarandas in the third section of the Home section. Not what you would call a prominent position. But she thought this was a neat idea. She cut it out and put in on my desk and I took it and read it on the air at KSDO and gave the phone number for people to call.

Sylvia was deluged with people calling, saying, "I love this idea."

At home, my wife Cindy said that this was something she wanted to do. "We are going to plant a tree in my Dad's memory," she said. So I went again on the air and talked about how we were going to sponsor a tree.

Sylvia got hundreds of calls. She called to thank us and I put her on the air. She got deluged again.

At one of my KSDO remote broadcasts from the 1993 Del Mar Fair a gardener came forward with his 90-plus year-old grandfather. "My grandfather was Kate Sessions' driver," he said. "And I'm the gardener who plants the Jacarandas."

A month later, Sylvia came to my KSDO remote broadcast at McCormick and Schmick's in Pacific Beach. She was coming to give a progress report and was in line to get on the air. During a break she felt dizzy and moved to the back of the restaurant. Her husband started taking her home but she felt worse, so they went straight to the hospital. There she had a stroke and died.

But the dream of Jacarandas for San Diego did not die with her. Sylvia Simpson Coleman's vision is being carried on by others, particularly her friend Donna Derrick. The Village Garden Club has worked with Caltrans and the Park and Recreation Department. They have planted more than 150 trees.

Near the Visitor's Center at Mission Bay Park is a small grove of Jacarancas and a bench dedicated to Sylvia Simpson Coleman, who has become a hero not for leading a political movement or for righting an injustice, but for believing in and fighting for one thing only -

beauty. May the annual San Diego Jacaranda Festival be Sylvia's legacy to the power of the dedicated individual.

Wipe Out Graffiti

The first time Rosie Bystrak called the show, I knew that this was a busy woman. There were kids in the background raising a ruckus and she was adamant. She had been on vacation with her family and was coming home when they drove by Third Avenue in Chula Vista. It was her favorite street in town, filled with charming shops and older buildings. It had been attacked with graffiti.

"I've had it with graffiti in Chula Vista" she said. "This is just incredible. These little punks are taking over our neighborhood and intimidating people and making us feel like we are under siege in our own communities."

"I agree with you," I said. "This is a problem that obviously the government doesn't have an answer for. People talk about it but nothing much is happening. What are you going to do about it?"

"You know what," she said. "I'm going to organize a paint-out. This Saturday, I challenge your listeners to meet me at the Chula Vista Community Center to help. I'm going to get some donated paint and I'm going to get organized."

And she did.

Rosie called back, kids still playing all around her in the background, and said, "O.K. We got the paint, we got the brushes, we have the Boy Scouts helping us, the Garden Club and the PTA. We're going to do this."

And they did.

"We had our first organizational meeting on Sunday afternoon, May 5. Since it was a holiday, I wasn't expecting anyone, but we had 30 people volunteering to help!" said Rosie. She had put out a simple flyer around town calling for a Graffiti Wipe-Out. She didn't have a computer, she didn't have spell-check, she just sat down and did it. It read:

Dear Neighbors,

The time has come for neighbors to get together and combat the violations put upon us by wreckless youth that doesn't respect law and order both public or private.

I'm a concerned citizen who is appalled by the sudden rash of *graffitti* all over our beautiful city of Chula Vista and adjoining communities. A public meeting will be held in your behalf so you can address your concerns and hopefully we as neighbors can work together and take back what is rightfully ours.

If you cannot come, please send someone in your behalf. Another way you can help, is if you can pass along this information to friends or relatives who are equally as concerned as yourself. This is a grassroots effort.

Cordially Yours,

Your neighbor

So the next thing I knew, Rosie had the politicians involved and now there is a Chula Vista Graffiti Ordinance. She is networking with

South Bay Community Services and the Correctional Behavior Institute of San Diego to get troubled kids to come out and do the paint-out. She organized into an official group — Citizens Against Graffiti.("I wanted to call it Neighbors Against Graffiti," she admitted, "NAG.")

Now Rosie goes once a month into the schools to recruit students to come to the paint-out. She works hand in hand with the Public Works Deptment in Chula Vista to match paint with public walls and set priorities in painting. Supervisor Brian Bilbray's office staff and many staff members the City Council know her by name.

And you know what? Graffiti is almost gone from Chula Vista. Citizens Against Graffiti's next project is to complete a manual on organizing an anti-graffiti campaign that other areas can use. They wrote the book.

Meanwhile, as all these housewives and families were out painting the walls with their kids trailing behind them, they realized that there is not enough day care in Chula Vista. Rosie is now on a campaign to open a day care facility in an historic home in her beloved city, combining two important projects into one.

She'll do it.

The point is, once you get started on one thing, you see that you can do more and more. Rosie was a spark plug and determined to make a change in her community. She didn't have expertise, training, a secretary or funding. Yet she was able to accomplish something that thousands of dollars of taxes and hours of bureaucratic timewasting was unable to do. And never would.

Silent No More

Cherie Chandler was similar to Rosie in her outrage. When President Clinton announced at the beginning of his term that his number one priority was opening up the military to homosexuals, everything hit the fan. I had lots of callers with lots of comment, but no one really said they were going to do anything about it.

Then Cherie called. She said, "I just can't believe that after all he said about the economy, this is the first thing Clinton is doing."

I said, "What are you going to do about it?"

She said, "I'm going to organize a group. We're going to write everybody and demonstrate against it and make sure our legislators never vote for it."

I said, "That's great. What are you going to call this group?"

She said, "I've been thinking about it and I've come up with this name. I think it really nails who we are and what we want and where we are coming from. The name is: Silent No More.

I flipped out. Everybody understands this phrase.

Richard Nixon won his 1972 election by appealing to the Silent Majority and saying, "Don't let the activists run this country. Elect me, I'm one of you."

Silent No More appeals to those who are ready to do something. There are lots of people saying, "Yeah, I don't agree with this crap that's going on, but it's somebody else's problem."

Cherie Chandler said, "No, it's our problem, we're Silent No More and we are going after this."

We were deluged with phone calls. Cherie got all the numbers and started to organize. In fact, she had already been thinking about how she wanted to shape the group. She tells the story like this:

"I agonized for weeks about whether or not to call Roger because I'd heard him enough to know that he'd turn it around back to me. I didn't call him until I felt sure that I was ready to act," she said.

Her first organizational meeting saw an impressive group of professionals and concerned citizens volunteering to help with the effort. Cherie laid out the parameters of her vision, emphasizing that they would act with dignity toward the issue of gays in the military, not allowing hatred or prejudice or derogatory remarks, but with the firm belief that Clinton's policy would be a mistake.

Next, the group adopted priorities and broke into committees — T-shirts, fund-raising, telephoning and more.

"Lots of people with computers wanted to start a newsletter right away," said Cherie. "But I felt that a telephone tree was more personal, less costly and just as effective. You don't need to be spending lots of money to make an impact."

The group decided that a petition drive would be the first activity they would undertake. For five weeks, this steering group met to plan their strategies.

Finally, they held their rally. The T-shirts were ready for sale, the petitions were printed and Congressman Duncan Hunter was the speaker. All of their organizational work paid off. Over 200 people rallied to their cause and the petition drive got a jump start.

Cherie started a bank account, considering Silent No More a club with the view of only raising money for postage and the mail box. But money poured in. People sent in money just by hearing the name. Silent No More resonated throughout the county. And the volunteers stand ready to get involved when the next threatening issue stirs them to action.

"People at work would hear about what I was doing and they couldn't believe it," said Cherie. "'What are you doing?' they would ask. 'Why are you doing all this work? You can't make a difference.'

"'Well, for one thing, we wouldn't even be here in the country if people long ago didn't think that their actions could make a difference,' I told them. 'For instance, is there anybody left who doesn't know what MADD is? One woman whose one daughter was killed in one small town started something that has changed laws in every city throughout the entire United States. If she can do that, why can't I?" said Cherie.

And why can't you?

Chapter Six

Blow The Whistle, Blow Your Job

*To sin by silence, when we should protest,
makes cowards out of men...
The few who dare must speak and speak again
to right the wrongs of many.*
—Ella Wheeler Wilcox, 1914

If, within the last year, you've listened to my KSDO Community Forum at all, picked up any one of my newsletters or heard me speak on any occasion, you probably recognize the name David Sossaman. If you've read my first book, *If We Say It Enough We'll Believe It,* then you know his story.

Briefly, David Sossaman is a former National City police officer who retired on disability from the force after being injured in an accident at the end of a high-speed chase. He has survived three shoot-outs and many, many dangerous encounters. David is a very courageous individual.

After leaving the police force, David went to work as an investigator in the Welfare Fraud division of the County Department of Social Services. For three years he watched with dismay as illegal aliens invaded the welfare offices with phony residency papers, welfare workers paid themselves by setting up bogus accounts, welfare workers sold their clients drugs and Mexican girls crossed the border to give birth to be able to go back home and pick up welfare checks in San Ysidro for the next 18 years.

Do The Right Thing

Finally David Sossaman blew the whistle. He called me on KSDO and told me that he could prove that 60 percent of the Aid to Families with Dependent Children (AFDC) recipients were frauds. That was $200 million dollars a year in fraud!

At first there was a show of cooperation. The Welfare Fraud

Division was allowed by Social Services to do a surprise audit in the Oceanside office — the furthest from the border you can get. Even so, he was right. He found over 60 percent of their files included fraud.

The head of Social Services, Jake Jacobson, came on my show and denied everything.

David went to the Grand Jury, who did an investigation and David and other investigators did more audits. The Grand Jury concluded that at least $70 million was fraud.

Jake Jacobson lost his job.

Then David encountered the problem of missing files. More than 6,000 of them. Monthly checks were going out to more than 6,000 people who had no files. An anonymous caller tipped him off to some hidden files in an administrators office. Things got very tense.

The Grand Jury got even more upset. Here was evidence of fraud and cover-up. Meanwhile, David was receiving threatening phone calls at home and all kinds of harassment. He went on Dan Rather's and Dianne Sawyer's news programs and became nationally known as a whistleblower for welfare fraud.

Then, David Sossaman lost his job.

And so my listeners did an amazing thing. We want to hire David, they said on the air. We want to put up the money so he can continue his investigation, anyway. We'll donate some money and he'll work for us. And that's exactly happened. David was financed by caring people who believed in his integrity until he could find another job. The people who call radio a "passive medium" have never listened to my listeners!

And the welfare fraud continues. Shortly after this, San Diego County Supervisors voted to have all welfare fraud investigators transferred to the authority of the District Attorney's office. This was a start. Then newly-elected Supervisor Dianne Jacob asked for a state audit of our welfare department and this, almost a year later, has yet to be accomplished.

In addition to that, Supervisors Dianne Jacob and Pam Slater in 1993 appointed David Sossaman to the Social Services Advisory Board. This had been a citizens advisory group to the welfare department for many years, but had always been a quiet voice.

Well, with Dave on the board, all a sudden they were investigating MediCal fraud, employment practices and all these things that he had discovered when he was an employee of the department.

Then Dick Rider was put on the board and between the two of them they started going after some of these irregularities. Unfortunately, the bureaucracy didn't like this, so they shut it down.

The cynics among us are justified in our cynicism when, as part of the $2 billion budget of the County of San Diego, the $30,000 or so spent on secretarial services for the citizen oversight committee was cut and, in the name of cutting the budget, the group disbanded. The members offered to meet without secretarial support, but Chairman Brian Bilbray stopped their involvement completely.

A Happy Ending

One of the positive results of Sossaman's action was, because he risked being an activist, blowing the whistle and saying what needed to be said about reform and fraud, he became a real hero. Not only did he singlehandedly bring about a Grand Jury investigation and the firing of the chief of the welfare department, he also got a tremendous job in the private sector. Dave now works with an insurance company to uncover physician and attorney fraud. He is making more money and is happier than ever doing the same thing in the private sector. Sometimes you fight city hall and win big.

Meanwhile, Over At MediCal

Rob Miller came to my attention when he called KSDO and said he wanted to talk about MediCal fraud.

A young law student, Rob Miller was working his way through school in a job as a benefits analyst with MediCal. He is very anglo-looking, with fair coloring, and most of his clients had no idea that he was fluent in Spanish. Over and over he would hear his clients come in and talk in Spanish about the office that gave out "free money." And as many times as the Social Services Department said that there were no illegals on welfare, Rob Miller knew better.

I invited him to come on my show. He knew that it would make this superiors very unhappy, but he couldn't take it any longer. Out of his normal case load of 500 cases he knew that most of them involved fraud. Miller blew the whistle on the air at KSDO and his reward was a termination notice for "not carrying out his duties."

We Don't Like Your Kind

The day after the broadcast, Miller returned to work to find:

- File cabinets with all 500 of his case files had been removed from his office.

- His computer access code was changed, locking him out of the computer system.

- He had to turn over his voice mail code so that his incoming calls could be monitored.

- He was relieved of all duties and required to label empty folders all day and do other clerical tasks.

These were not standard procedures for terminated employees of the department. In fact, according to David Sossaman, employees of Social Services who were being investigated for fraud, including an admitted heroin addict, did not have these types of actions taken against them.

I was so incensed by this outrage I asked Rob Miller to write up his story and I had thousands printed and distributed through The Roger Report and other outlets. Here are highlights of the Rob Miller story in his own words as it appeared in The Roger Report:

The Rob Miller Story - In His Own Words

I enjoy the Hispanic culture and like to socialize in Tijuana. Prior to working with the County, I recall that at some parties I heard

Mexicans boasting about how the U.S. Government paid for their mother's new pacemaker or some other operation. I could never understand how they could possibly do it and I though they were exaggerating. After spending a few months at MediCal, I realize they were telling the truth. Sometimes, now, if I am at a friend's house in Mexico, people ask me if MediCal can find out if they own property in Mexico. I always tell them "yes" to discourage them from applying for welfare.

I believe our welfare system encourages illegal immigration into this country. And MediCal, where I work, is usually the first introduction to the welfare system. Of all welfare programs, it is the most easy to receive and probably the most expensive program to operate. All a person has to do is be alive, physically present in the State of California with the intention to stay, and prove they are medically needy.

All MediCal recipients have to show how they are meeting their needs. They can't just say, "I get by." Some applicants are afraid to report income because it will make them ineligible for benefits or will make them at risk to pay taxes. In this case, MediCal needs a sworn statement from the provider.

When I first started working for MediCal I would use the computer to cross-reference the names of people who said they provided rent, utilities and clothing for my clients. I discovered that most of the providers living in the same household were on welfare themselves. If that provider's file was in our office, I would check and find that *my* client was listed as the provider for them. Even worse, sometimes the absent parent in that household would sign the provider's statement for my client and the absent parent in my case would sign for them.

Without question, the thrust of the department is to make sure that recipients receive their benefits, not to discourage fraud. When I first arrived for MediCal training I knew that something was up because I was told to keep a variety of colored pens and pencils at my desk. That way I could fill in the blanks with the same color ink that the client had used.

There is a standing joke in the Department of Social Services that we should simply open a welfare office in Tijuana. That way we won't inconvenience our border-crossing clients. We laughed about putting a welfare kiosk right on the border so they could drive up on the Mexican side and get their checks and food stamps, then they would be another window where they could cash their checks.

In my own way I put up a defense against fraud. I always scheduled my appointments as early as possible, in hopes that my clients would be too lazy to cross the border so early in the morning.

One intake worker told me that when they spot a fake ID they are supposed to accept it as valid. The latest rumor I heard on the job was that blank Puerto Rican birth certificates were found in one of the worker's desk.

The greater frustration is that after spending time and effort to refer the case and have the investigation unit confirm the fraud, the worker is routinely instructed to leave the case open and continue benefits. The justification is given that the case will be re-opened anyway after an appeal. This is, unfortunately, true. Administrative appeal judges almost always rule in favor of the client. One worker told me that although she was told to deny a case not once but three times by welfare investigators, she was still made to grant the case.

Why shouldn't illegal aliens come across the border for assistance? They get better medical care here, their children will have dual citizenship, their chances are better for getting green card and they'll never go hungry.

Is This Government Health Care?

MediCal in San Diego County is a program out of control and Rob Miller's whistle-blowing set off a series of investigative reports in other media. Not only do we have stories of poor illegals abusing the system, we now know that rich people come here from other countries for free medical care, too. As documented in a series of articles in the San Diego Union-Tribune, rich foreigners from as far away as Russia have ripped off MediCal.

Nothing in the Clinton Health Care Plan would stop this fraud. It would simply make it easier for people to participate in the system. Everyone working in the United States will get a health card. They are not going to ask if you are legal or illegal any more than they do right now. And another five million people will be carried on the welfare roles by taxpayers like you and me.

Grandpa Goes to High School

Treasure Love, a clerk at Crawford High School in the San Diego Unified School District, had a problem. Day after day she would see records of groups of Somali and other refugee students supposedly enrolled in school but were not attending. These students were registered as being 16 - 18 years old, but many of them had the same birthday, January 1.

After some investigation, it was discovered that these students were not teenagers at all, in fact, some of them were grey-haired grandpas. But they did have one thing in common, they were all receiving welfare. The welfare department accepts school enrollment as proof of eligibility for AFDC.

Love knew fraud when she saw it, so she brought this to the attention of the school district and welfare fraud personnel in October of 1992. Meetings were held then, more meetings were held with the District Attorney's Fraud Division in May of 1993, more meetings were held in July of 1993. Finally, in October 1993, a year later, it was on the agenda at the joint Board of Supervisor/School Boards meeting.

But what happened to Love? She was demoted - "reassigned" - to stamping books and cleaning out old files because, according to Crawford Principal David LeMay, she did not show "sensitivity to multi-cultural differences."

If you're talking about the cultural difference between obeying the law in a foreign country and coming here illegally to rip off a lazy public school at the taxpayers expense, then I think there are some differences we just can't tolerate.

In October 1993, this same fraud came to light at Mountain Empire School District, where administrators send buses to the border at Tecate to bring Mexican kids to the schools every morning. We are not talking about a few dozen refugee "kids" anymore. We are talking about almost 400 children coming into the school district on a daily basis getting a free education to the tune of over $1 million per year. Of your money.

It's getting to be a familiar dance. The schools blame the Border Patrol, the Border Patrol blames the legislators, the legislators blame whoever they can find to blame. Meanwhile, the Average Daily Attendance (ADA) figures go up, state money pours into the schools and everyone winks at the fraud.

Everybody Put Your Lips Together

Now is the time for more David Sossamans, Rob Millers and Treasure Loves to take a stand. As this book goes to press, a strong new ordinance protecting whistleblowers has been passed by the San Diego County Board of Supervisors calling for a citizen's review commission that would receive information from whistleblowers and to review their allegations.

Chapter Seven

You Can't Win Them All

There is no credit in being a comedian,
when you have the whole government working for you.
All you have to do is report the facts.
I don't even have to exaggerate.
—Will Rogers, 1935

In September, 1993, Katie Zolezzi wrote me a letter saying, "I quit! The city wins, I'm shutting down. I can't make enough money to operate my business under the restrictions, rules, policies and regulations that the City of San Diego has insisted upon. I give up!"

Katie, Director of the Art Center in Mission Hills, has put up a good fight. She started her business to make up for the total elimination of art training in the public schools. She started her business to provide day care for some of the more than 5,000 children who are in year-round schooling with no available care during their 6-8 week breaks. She started her business because she cared about quality of life and art training for kids in San Diego.

But when Katie Zolezzi first brought her story to me over a year ago, she had already been through two years of a bureaucratic nightmare and had spent over $20,000 fighting City Hall. All she wanted to do was move to a larger facility and serve more kids. Ultimately, Katie won that battle. Now, 12 months later, she feels she has lost the war.

Why bring it up here? After all, isn't this book about beating the bureaucrats?

Know When To Fold 'Em

First of all, I want to make it clear that among our citizen "heroes," Katie is one of the most courageous. As you will read in this chapter, she has had far more patience and persistence in dealing with more complete bureaucratic stupidity than anyone I've ever seen.

Secondly, if there is anyone left in San Diego who thinks that the nit-picking, inflexible, arrogant and overblown bureaucrats don't run the show, let them read on. Forget worrying about the wishes and desires of the public at large. The scary thing about this story is that despite direction from the city council and the mayor, despite the direction from even another bureaucracy set up specifically to deal with day care problems, despite the best intentions of all kinds of people, no one has been able to untangle the web of regulation that has strangled Katie Zolezzi and her Art Center.

Finally, this story is important to read because there comes a time when you may have to retreat. There comes a time when you have to step back, regroup and acknowledge that the power you are up against is massive and overwhelming.

But don't let it stop there. Complain to everybody in politics about your defeat, write letters about your defeat, tell reporters about your defeat, scream about your defeat.

This is Katie Zolezzi's scream.

A Losing Battle

Katie's letter to city officials, (reprinted below) tells in eloquent language the struggle of the Art Center to operate in compliance with all the city rules and regulations. It was written about one year after Katie began her effort to become licensed for day care. Read and weep.

October 3, 1991

To: Honorable Maureen O'Connor - Mayor of San Diego

Councilman John Hartley - Hillcrest District

Councilman Ron Roberts - Mission Hills District

Ms. Alda Yribe - Community Care Licensing

Ms. Pam Raptis - Hazardous Materials Management

Ms. Pat Grabsky - San Diego Zoning Division

Ms. Leona De Paepe - Deputy Fire Marshall

Mr. Tom Pazant - Superintendent, San Diego Unified

Ms. Kay Wagner - Art Manager, San Diego Unified

You have a serious problem you have failed to recognize. On one side of your campaigns you say there is a real need for "quality child care" in the San Diego area due to the rising numbers of duo-working parents and working single parent households, yet you have created and passed ordinances that have set criteria which are impossible to meet. As a result, you have all but eliminated any possibility to fulfill the needs of these working parents.

For the past year (which I thought was more than enough time) I have been trying to have my Art Center in Mission Hills licensed as a child care facility. Since I had one year left on my old lease and since the building I was in did not qualify for licensing, I felt I would be able to easily move into a new facility which would qualify. I attended a three-hour seminar on licensing and proceeded to begin filling out the appropriate forms to meet the "A1-A17" and "B1-13" requirements for Division 12, Chapter 1. I wanted to do the right thing!

It is relatively easy for me to get a child care permit in my home to attend babies and toddlers as a "baby sitter" but it is totally impossible for me to get a permit within a 10-15 mile radius of downtown San Diego, to offer weekly "Enrichment Art Programs" to the vast numbers of school-age children between 5 and 16 who attend year-round schools and are on vacation throughout the year.

I do not think you have realized or have addressed the issue that there are 3,000-5,000-plus children between the ages of 5-16 who are out of school each and every Monday throughout the school year. (Attached is a list of San Diego City Schools on the year-round schedules.) From June through September that number is even greater due to the traditional school summer vacation. Most working parents cannot take time off every nine weeks to keep their children off the streets and occupied. In spite of this vast number of vacationing mid-year children, there is relatively little offered for them to do. Children just "hang out" alone at home watching T.V. or perhaps get into trouble on the streets.

I had an "enrichment" alternative solution for some of these children, but I have been shut down and now forced out of business due to your General Licensing Requirements-Division 12-Chapter 1 and Ordinance #17657 passed June 24, 1991 after many delays.

Due to the requirements in Division 12, Chapter 1 and Ordinance #17657, I cannot find a suitable location anywhere near the downtown area of San Diego which will qualify. If I find a building with the inside space I need to meet the 35 square feet per child, it has no back yard to meet the 75 square feet of outside play area per child. To provide a program for just "48" children I would need a building with a minimum of 1680 square feet inside and 3600 square feet outside. Forty-eight children is not that many.

Perhaps if I am lucky, I will find a building with the minimum requirements, but it will probably be a house and not a commercial building, which lacks any play yard space. In addition to the inside-outside square footage, I must provide three bathrooms (1 for every 15 children) and a separate bathroom for the staff. Please tell me how many houses in Mission Hills, Hillcrest, North Park, Kensington, Downtown or Golden Hills have four bathrooms in a 1680 sq. ft. house? My residence is 2900 sq. ft. with three stories and we only have 2.5 bathrooms.

So, I must try again and move on to the next house, which, of course, must be located in a C-R zone or I have to get a conditional use permit which takes 6-10 months.

Now, stay with me on this. Maybe I can find the house with the bathrooms and perhaps the outside play area is fairly close in size, but the house has a second story. Children are not allowed to use the second story according to the Fire Marshal permits — so the bathrooms don't qualify. I have yet to find a house with four bathrooms on the first floor.

Let's say I am lucky again and I find a house which is zoned commercial-residential, has four bathrooms, is one story and has a nice play yard outside. Guess what...it doesn't have 4-6 parking places on the property. The only parking is street parking. Once again, it will not qualify.

O.K. Last, but not least, I *did* find a perfect building that had 1500 sq. ft. inside (good for 42.9 children) had a great play area outside, 1635 sq. ft. (good for only 21.8 children - even though they would not all be outside at the same time) and even had 6 parking spaces in the front, off the street AND it had three of the four bathrooms. And it was centrally located to uptown and downtown on Third Ave. So, you say, "Wow! Great! You did it!"

Wrong. It was next to the Dialysis Treatment Center and, in spite of their excellent record of disposal of their hazardous waste products, in spite of the fact that it is made of block with no windows, their dumpster is located in an enclosed locker inside their underground parking lot and the building is security locked at all times, I cannot lease the house next to it. (By the way, it took over four months to find out that this house wouldn't work.) At this point in time I am nearing the end of summer and have six weeks left on my existing lease. My frustration is mounting...

Parents call constantly asking for weekly art programs for their children while on "mid-year" vacation because these parents must work. Yet, according to your rules, requirements and ordinances, if a child attends more than six hours a week, we must have a child care license. As mentioned above, you have made that totally impossible. I am discouraged, depressed, extremely frustrated and angry!!

The old saying, "You Can't Fight City Hall," is very true. I give up! I have given this effort my best shot! I have an extra-large three-ring binder filled with forms, papers, floor plans, emergency procedures from three agencies and I have invested $1000 in a variety of fees, health screenings, TB testing for my staff and finger printing sent to Sacramento. All this takes time. I was recently told that the finger prints I had sent earlier were no longer valid due to the changing of my application from one address to another. I would have to re-file again at $35 per person.

I honestly feel you really don't care about the children in our community, nor do you care about their parents. Your ordinance #17657 is truly unreasonable. You have made the law as difficult as you possibly could make it! But I do not have $10,000 nor six to eight months to fight it, nor do I have any more energy. I am totally out of money and out of business because of this new ordinance. In addition, my staff of 12 teachers, assistants and office staff are out of work. But the truly most unfortunate victims in this whole mess are the children of San Diego.

Maybe this letter will wake you up to the needs of the people and especially the children and you will amend your ordinance to be more reasonable and workable.

Sincerely,

Katherine Zolezzi

Hurry Up And Wait

The deadline for Katie's lease arrangement came and went. She had to let go all of her employees and shut down her business. But she did not give up her fight as indicated. She had an encouraging meeting in November where it looked like the hazardous waste problem would be resolved and she could move into the building on Third Ave. It had formerly been a residence for the handicapped, so had already been screened through all kinds of regulations.

By Dec. 18, 1991 though, Katie was getting anxious. She decided another letter to the Mayor, City Council members with copies to several child care and planning agency bureaucrats might speed things along. Here is the text of that letter:

To: Honorable Mayor O'Connor and all Councilmembers

On Nov. 25, 1991, I came before you with the request that Ordinance 17657 relating to child care be amended to separate businesses which are required to have a Health Permit from the County Hazardous Materials Management Division, into classifications which are based on a toxic threshold rather than the general classification for which all now require a minimum of 150-ft. buffer zone for all businesses (there are over 75000) which have health permits.

I was led to believe on Nov. 25 from the encouraging vote (7:1:1) that this amendment would be corrected as soon as possible. I was told the procedure would take the Ordinance back to the Planning Department which would make it top priority, then to the Planning

71

Commission and back to the City Council in early January for a vote. I'm now told it will be January 28 — hardly early January. I was led to believe that the amendment would be corrected so that I could once again be open for business at my new location on Third Avenue. I was led to believe that I could open in early February. If that was true, it will be six months since I have been out of work, with no income, due to inaccurate wording in the Ordinance.

Yesterday I was talking with Ceci Hurtado of Councilman Behr's office. I was now told that it looks like mid-March before I will get a zoning permit and license. That means April before I can open again. Do you realize that you have now added two more months to my unemployment, my staff unemployment and the fact that my customers have been without my programs for 8 months? This is totally unreasonable! And all this frustration is for an error in wording which you all agreed was your mistake and must be corrected. Does it really take four months to make a correction? No wonder businesses move out of San Diego.

I have been fighting this Ordinance since the day after it was passed last June. For a new law which is supposed to simplify, it certainly has been complicated. If it gets corrected in March, then it will have taken a total of 10 months to correct. What can possibly take so long?

Due to the support you showed me on Nov. 25, I was lead to believe that I would be back in business in February. As a result, in good faith I have entered into a lease agreement on the Third Ave.

property with the buyer and seller. Now I wonder if I am going to be a tenant in a 'nothing' business, because I can't get my zoning permit until at least April 1. I cannot apply for my child care license without a lease. The processing for licensing takes time too. This whole issue has not affected just me and my family, but my staff. It has held up the sale of the property since February. Now it is late December and I am told there are four more months of possible delays of ahead.

Please, if it is at all possible in January, when the new amendment is accepted, may I get a temporary license or some sort of waiver so I can open my doors in February as planned while the rest of the crazy red-tape gets on the books and passed around to all the right offices? I do not feel that it is justified to hold me up an other six weeks due to this new paper shuffling. That is your responsibility — mine is to get my doors open again, get my staff back to work (if any are left) and get the children back into my programs.

Please do something today — not tomorrow — not April, 1992. We all agreed that the Dialysis Center is not a threat to the children. Let me open my doors February 1, 1992. It seems to me that if the Ordinance Amendment is accepted on January 28, I should be able to get my permit on January 29.

I have come too far now to quit! I cannot find another suitable location anywhere near Mission Hills or HIllcrest. This whole issue has become totally absurd! I have tried to be patient but my patience is running very, very thin. Would you like to reimburse me and my staff for the months of lost income? And you are all due a pay raise???

I am not a political activist — I just want to go back to doing what I do best, teaching children. Get me back to work and I promise never to bother you again.

Sincerely,

Katherine Zolezzi

Out Of the Frying Pan Into The Fire

Katie got then-County Supervisor Susan Golding to write to Mayor O'Connor as well for some kind of temporary approval to get her doors open, but there was no response. Finally the city allowed Katie to go ahead with moving into the property, but she was still not allowed to opeate the Art Center. She still had a long way to go.

The process of permit approval began with three fire inspectors checking the property. It passed all inspections. Five separate trips to the zoning department were made, each time Katie went they said that one more thing was missing from the file. A final inspection determined that her facility was four inches too close to the building next door.

She was told that her options were to either knock out the wall of her property ($30,000) or put up a "water wall" of fire sprinklers on the outside. Five city-approved sprinkler operators came to the property to give her estimates. None ever got back to her.

The city finally said that it didn't care anymore about the "water wall" but she had to fix all three exits. Katie asked for the city requirements in writing. It took 12 weeks to receive them.

Part of the requirements listed indicated that she had to rebuild the handicapped ramp going into the house. This was a surprise because the house had previously been a handicapped group home. If the ramp was O.K. for people in wheelchairs who used it every day, day in and day out, why was it not adequate for her, with no handicapped children or parents? She had to extend it so it would have a few degrees lower incline. To do that, she had to use up half of a parking space.

Finally, on August 21, 1992, Katie Zolezzi received permission to re-open her business. I was proud of her perseverance. It had taken a year and she had spent over $20,000 but she had won her fight against City Hall.

In the December 1992 issue of my newsletter, The Roger Report, Katie's story was reported and she told me, "I learned that the city council is tied up by the city manager's office. I feel like the only easy solution would be to build a child care facility in the middle of the desert and still I would probably have to make sure it was not near a landfill site."

Losing The War

One of the things that made the Third Ave. property appealing to Katie was the fact that there was a two-story building in the rear of the property that could accommodate more children. By Spring of 1993, she knew that she wanted to proceed to expand the Center. Here, in this final letter to me from Katie, is what happened:

Dear Roger,

My enrollment has grown to 30 full time children (my maximum) with 7-12 additional children at odd times so that I do not exceed my limit (i.e. mid-day kindergartners, art camps, etc.) I need more room. I currently have a waiting list, so I must be doing something right.

When I originally rented the property on Third Ave. I expected to eventually move into the back building to accommodate a larger enrollment. In May 1993, I began the steps to move into that building, as I am familiar now with how slowly the city operates. I wanted to have enough time to be ready by September enrollment.

According to the people in Building and Zoning, the back building, built around 1980, had to be modified up to '93 codes:

* Sprinkler system on the second floor
* Two new exits to the outside
* Close in walls, create new walls
* Change exit doors to open out and have emergency bars put on them
* Enlarge the toilet rooms by 1.5 to 2 feet
* Connect to an emergency alarm system
* Seal off storage area under the stairs.

My landlord, out of good faith for me, hired an architectural designer to see what could be done to accommodate all these requirement within a reasonable money limit. As it turned out, in order to do what the city wanted it would cost over $35,000.

This was totally out of the question! Not only is this unreal for a child care remodel (tuition is $135 a month) but the two new exits would take away 50 percent of my play area.

So I decided to only use the downstairs area. At least I could add 20 children. To do this, I was told by Structural Engineering, all I had to do was fix the exits, tie into an alarm company and seal off the stairway storage so it could not be used. I could plead a "hardship" on the two bathrooms and not have to enlarge them. O.K. Done! So I thought. Ha!

Now I went back to the city to finalize the paperwork and get my permit. It was now August 1992.

Guess what? I now find out from Zoning that I am short 1/2 of a parking place. (Remember the handicapped ramp?) I'm supposed to have 5 spaces. I took them a picture of my parking with 5 cars on it. Not good enough! Seems my whole parking lot is illegal. It shouldn't be there at all and, if it were acceptable, it would have to be paved, not gravel.

I talked to Deb Ferrin the Child Care Coordinator for the City of San Diego who is supposed to "fast track" these kinds of requests. She suggested a meeting with all the parties involved. On Friday, Sept. 17, 1993 I met with Deb Ferrin, Jim Churchill, Structural Engineering Senior; Sam Oats, Assistant Fire Marshal; Karen Flarety, Zoning; Burch Ertle, Senior Zoning and Ann Van Leer from Councilman Ron Roberts office.

In one breath, according to the city people the two buildings are separate with two separate addresses. The front building is 1500 sq. ft. and the downstairs in the back is around 750 sq. ft. I had to pay separately for two different permits. However, in the parking issue, they lump both buildings together. Originally they accepted the tandem parking for the front building, but now they say they never should have OK'd these spots. If the two buildings are viewed separately, I have enough parking. With the two buildings judged together, I need to have another 1/2 space. Mr. Ertle is adamant and won't give an inch.

Instead Ertle suggested that I request a "discretionary parking permit variance" from the Center City Planning District for $2,650. This money would buy a request — they could still say "No" and I would be out the money.

"This is out of the question," I told them. "I don't have any money."

"Well!" he said, "perhaps you can get an 'alternative compliance review' for only $1450." In this case notices would be sent to all my neighbors near the center and maybe it would be O.K. That's 11 monthly tuitions for 1/2 a parking space.

In the meantime, Mr. Churchill, who earlier in the meeting said I had met all of his requirements, was bored and thumbing through his huge regulation manual to pass the time. All of a sudden he sits up straight, interrupts the debate over the 1/2 parking space and asks, "What kind of roof do you have on the two buildings?"

I haven't a clue. It was never brought up in three years. Suddenly, it seems that I must have a "class B" roof on both buildings. He found a new way to make my life miserable.

All this time, Ann Van Leer from the Councilman's office has said little to nothing. But she took tons of notes.

When the meeting was adjourned, these city power brokers had the silly idea that I was going to pay either $2650 or $1450 for some kind of variance or compliance review, put on a new roof and make some kind of "lot tie agreement" with my landlord. I'm sure they all felt very smugly that the meeting had gone well.

Ann Van Leer rode down the elevator with me. She said she now understood what I have been going through since this all started in August of 1990.

Needless to say, I am very discouraged. I don't have a dime extra to spend on all these new improvements. I have borrowed money from as many "former" friends as I can.

THE CITY HAS WON THIS BATTLE! My lease is up in February of 1995, if I last that long. I think I will toss in the towel and not renew my option. I can't make money at this business with all these unnecessary expenses.

I have five usable parking places. I have a great roof on both buildings (not shake) and they don't leak. I have made the doors safe and have smoke detectors in all the rooms in both buildings. There are many exits. I care about "my kids" and am a good teacher. I'm picky about my staff and only hire the best. I'm giving kids art experiences that they will never get anywhere else in their lives. I just can't spend money on a 1/2 parking space and a new roof. To fight City Hall you have to have a lot of money and a lot of time. As a small business owner, I have neither.

Thirty families will have to find a new child care facility whose owner is independently wealthy and only operates a child care center for something to pass the time. Perhaps they will hire me to do what I do best — teach children. I have no intention of continuing in politics.

Sincerely,

Katie Zolezzi

It's Not Over 'Til It's Over

As of this writing, Katie has not given up. She is still fighting. Unlike those "underground" day care centers, Katie is playing by the rules — and being driven to ruin by the bureaucracy that enforces the rules.

Stop the Press

It is the day before the book goes to press. Katie Zolezzi called me to say, "I've won! I had to be a crybaby, a brat and a whiner, but I've won my permit!"

Whether it's the influence of Councilman Ron Roberts and his hard-working assistant Ann Van Leer, the persistent support of my KSDO listeners or the sheer determination of Child Care Coordinator Deb Ferrin, I don't know. But at the last minute, Katie was awarded her permit. In addition, she received a personal phone call from City Manager Jack McGrory apologizing for the behavior of his underlings and was assured that she would be able to proceed with her use of the downstairs of the back building. She's in business!

"I've won," said Katie, "but I feel like I've been a misbehaving child for three years. The real tragedy is that I couldn't act like a reasonable adult and get them to do what was right."

Then she told me the Art Center had just been visited by a city landscaper who told her that to really be in compliance she needed to have more plants and trees, a three foot hedge in front and "according to the permit code..."

Chapter Eight

Digging
For Gold

*A government which robs Peter to pay Paul
can always depend on the support of Paul.*
—George Bernard Shaw, 1944

One of the greatest sources of strength for any bureaucracy is the monopolization of information regarding its own operation — its budget, its expenditures and its regulations. Not many people understand that.

Unless you know where and how to look for it, every bureaucracy will try to hide from the public how much money it actually has in its coffers. The written budget of any level of government is always a document designed to prevent you from understanding where it gets its money, how much is has now and how much it actually spends it. This may sound extreme to those, again, who carry around in their head a high school civics class vision of what American government is supposed to be. Believe me, in practice, in 1994, we have come 180 degrees away from that ideal. The tax revolt in California (which culminated in the passage of Proposition 13 in 1978 and was followed in subsequent elections by attempts to limit overall government spending in California) was a revolt that failed.

Actual revenues from the Prop. 13-limited property taxes doubled in the County of San Diego within ten years. At the same time, bureaucratic and political rhetoric would have you believe that the schools and local government services were crippled by Prop. 13, that you greedy homeowners had taken the money from the government services which was vital to a civilized community.

What really happened? In the 1980s, San Diego went through a real estate boom. So much new construction came on line it pushed up property tax revenues. People moved around and moved up so their properties were reassessed at some of the highest assessed values in local history.

Today, lesss than 10 percent of the homes are still inhabited by the same people who owned them in 1978. The other 90 percent have been re-appraised. Until the recent drop in values, all of this activity resulted in an absolute torrent of new property tax revenue pouring into local government in San Diego County. During the 1980s, the total budget for the City of San Diego doubled while the population only increased by 24 percent.

Even if you understand the financial information contained in the budget documents of local governments and agencies, this does not tell the full story of how much money local governments, special districts, school districts, city councils and the boards of supervisors have. Budgets do not document how much money has been hoarded and kept from the public, even while those politicians and bureaucrats continue to whine for more money and higher taxes, and threaten to cut libraries, park and recreation, law enforcement and other high priority services until they get higher taxes out of you.

I Have A Hunch

Bonnie Kibbee is a concerned citizen who understood this process more than most people and determined to dig until she found the evidence to support what her instinct told her existed. She continued to dig into water districts, city, county and state bank accounts until she had undeniable proof.

What Bonnie Kibbee found is an extraordinary tale, told here for the first time. Except for *The Roger Report* newsletter, this information has never been printed by the Union-Tribune or seen the light of day on any of the radio or television so-called "news coverage." Yet it is the kind of information that you must understand before you are able to knowledgeably participate in our democratic process. You need to know how much money these government agencies are really hiding.

Here is Bonnie Kibbee's tale in her own words:

Just Ask

I heard a rumor about two years ago that the Padre Dam Water District had millions of dollars in a bank account. Then I heard it more than once. There were two or three people mentioning it and it seemed to be a kind of accepted but little-known fact.

One day I'm going to stop by their office and ask how much cash they have, I thought to myself.

And one day I did. I went into the office of the Padre Dam Water District and asked the woman at the desk if she could tell me how much cash the District had in the bank. Within ten minutes they sent out the head of their bookkeeping department.

"What do you want to know for?" asked the head of bookkeeping.

"How much do you have?" I asked.

"Giving you a financial report will take days," he said.

"No," I said, "I just want the total. I'm not leaving until I have it."

In about ten minutes he came back to the front of the office. "There's

$42 million," he said.

He handed me a statement that showed the balance and where the money was invested.

If they have money, I thought, the Otay Water District must have money too. A friend of mine got their statement for me. At the time they had $75 million. The majority of it was invested in U.S. Treasury Bills in accounts ranging in terms from 30 days to 10 years.

I happened to mention this to my friend — and county employee — Sal Bua and he told me where to check. "Look into the Transnet accounts, which are held by SANDAG," he said, referring to the San Diego Association of Governments.

At that, I asked Bill Reichenbach to go with me. We went to SANDAG's offices at 10 a.m. and said we wanted a copy of their cash accounts. We sat by the front door until 5 p.m. and people were starting to leave. They had all kinds of excuses for us — they were busy, in meetings and on the phone. Finally they handed us a financial statement but it did not reflect a cash bank account. It was a budget, not a real picture of their finances.

Finally, Greg Scott of SANDAG met with me. It turned out they had $250 million in the Transnet account. While I was at it, I asked to see the Caltrans account. Mr. Scott got their capital outlay summary of funds available. It showed $3.2 billion for projects for the state of California.

How is it possible, I wondered, that we are paying all these taxes and there's all this money hoarded, but there are no jobs and no projects being built by these agencies?

I was starting to get it.

Next I went to the County of San Diego. Remember, the government only gives you what you ask for and I didn't know what to ask for exactly. First I asked a clerk for the total cash in the bank. Then she let a comment slip that made it all clear.

"Are you talking about the money pool?" she said.

I said, "Absolutely! I want a copy of everything in it."

I didn't really believe what I was hearing. It turned out the County of San Diego had cash accounts just short of $3 billion. Yes, the same county government that is always short of money for the Sheriff and other vital services had $3 billion in cash.

Whose Money Is It?

I made an appointment to see Bill Kelly in the County Auditor/ Comptroller's office at 10 a.m. I asked for the total cash in the money pool and whose accounts they were. He was very nice and helpful and said it would be ready later that day. It was. Kelly gave me books of information with a complete list of every bank account in the county. He even made a set of labels made for me so I could keep the files organized.

Finally I went to the City of San Diego. "Do you have any money?" I asked. City Treasurer Connie Jamison was extremely helpful. She handed me the statement for City of San Diego: $1 billion.

And in all of my dealings with all of these office workers, they told me that no one had ever asked for this information before. No councilmembers, no supervisors, no mayor, no activist goups. No one in the history of San Diego hnd simply asked, "How much money do you really have?"

Where Is All This Money?

The next question I wanted to ask was, "Where is all of this money?" I decided to pay a visit to Paul Boland, Treasurer of the County of San Diego. It was an important meeting and one where I finally said, "I think its time that this money be spent as intended to create jobs and turn the economy around."

Paul Boland replied, "Well, Bonnie. I've been after them for years as to why they haven't spent this money. Sixty percent of this money never leaves the account."

He looked at me, smiled and said, "I have something that will help you."

The document that Paul Boland gave me showed the accounting over 10 years where the cash reserves for the County went from $600,000 to almost $3 billion.

I thought to myself, You're on to something.

At that point I went on KSDO and talked to Roger about the money I'd found. He couldn't believe it.

Now I had the attention of Richard Gann, Chairman of the Paul Gann Citizen Committee, who hired me to help with a ninety-day investigation of money pools at the state level.

This was when I first heard the term "arbitrage." And this is when I finally figured out why this hoarding was taking place. The bureaucrats were hoarding the money to gain the interest since part of the interest into the General Fund. The bureaucrats were financing themselves from interest on capital project money so the capital projects could not being built!

We studied every county in California. Locally, it was found that in the year previous to our investigation, the money pool balance in San Diego had increased by $1 billion. The combined balances of the water district cash reserves was $600,000. The combined balances of all the cities in the county — $2 billion.

State Of California

Our investigation has proof that California state cash reserves have increased in 10 years from $5 billion to more than $24 billion. That's a 486% increase! In just the last six months of 1993, in the worst recession we've ever known, the state money pool has increased by more than $3 billion. In a state Governor Pete Wilson says can't balance its budget without increases!

All in all, statewide, we have already documented $75 billion in money pools, and estimate that the final figure will be double that amount.

Nobody Can Believe It

It was time to go back to Roger. I went on his show with my findings and they were printed in his newsletter, ***The Roger Report***, with a graph showing the increases. That's when I heard the scariest thing of all. Roger Hedgecock, former county supervisor and former mayor, said, "I never knew about this money. In all my years in politics, I never had any indication that this money existed."

Since then I have begun to meet with others. Sherry Curtis, Richard Gann and I met with several state politicians in Sacramento. They, too, couldn't believe what we were saying. They didn't think such funds existed.

"I have the account numbers and balances for every account in the state," I said.

"We'll look into it," they said.

Meanwhile, I have been able to get a Republican Party Resolution passed calling on Gov. Pete Wilson to get the money out of these accounts and back into the economy. U.S. Congressmen "Duke" Cunningham and Duncan Hunter are now sending letters to various state agencies asking, "What are all these designated funds designated for?"

And when are we going to start giving it back to the taxpayers instead of asking for more?

It's Just Begun

What a story! Bonnie Kibbee's simple question has uncovered a scandal in funding that is going to rock the state. This fight against "City Hall" has just started. Kibbee is writing a book including all of her findings, the numbers of the accounts, the balances, the charts and all of the other information that she has researched. It will be available in early 1994. For now, she continues to speak to groups throughout the county and state, letting everyday taxpayers know how much the supposed "bankrupt" government bodies really have in cash.

This is a fight that is just getting going. This one will be fun to win.

Chapter Nine

It's The
Taxes Stupid

*We shall tax and tax,
and spend and spend, and elect and elect.*
—Harry L. Hopkins, 1938

The Presidential election of 1992 focused the American voters' attention on the federal debt and deficit as no other election in our history had ever done. And well it should have. The annual deficit in 1992 exceeded the amount it took to win WWII. The total debt, at $4 trillion, is more than the gross domestic product of the whole United States of America for one year. We couldn't repay it if we stopped doing anything else but repay the debt, including eating.

The interest to pay the $4 trillion is now such a large part of the budget that it is only exceeded by the amount spent on defense. It is an amount equal to all of the personal income taxes paid by every American citizen west of the Mississippi river.

To whom do we owe this debt? We owe most of it to ourselves, if we own pensions or investment accounts or mutual funds. We owe some of it to foreign investors. We owe some of it to banks, which now buy a lot of federal debt because they can make more money from it than from lending money to business. Which is a big problem. Which is why we are not creating jobs. All the banks are lending money to the government and that keeps the regulators off their backs.

This kind of true financial crisis is comparable in our history only to the end of the Civil War when the currency was in danger of collapse. Even so, this federal debt and deficit issue would not have been fully debated between the Republican and Democratic parties if it were not for Ross Perot.

Let Me Show You A Chart

Ross Perot raised the issue of debt and deficit, raised the issue of its long-term and short-term impacts, raised the issue of why it was happening and put forward his own program of how to stop it. At that point his popularity soared because he was addressing an issue that most Americans felt had been neglected—it's like waking up in the morning and realizing that your credit card is so overdrawn that you actually have to do something.

So, what was the solution? The solution boiled down to really two—increase taxes and/or cut spending. Ultimately, every American knew that both of those would probably happen. But there was a war on in the 1992 Presidential election over which side you would take, because it revealed two different philosophies of government.

One political philosophy said, "Government is doing such important work that the cost of government is inevitably going to expand and the work it is doing is so vital that there is no way to meaningfully cut it. We have to raise taxes to meet the growing expenses of these necessary programs."

The other philosophy said, "Lot of what government does is wasteful, fraudulent and abusive. It ought to be stopped, it ought to be cut, it doesn't need to be done. The first objective ought to be to cut spending, in order to lower the deficit."

The "cut spending" group came mostly from the grass roots taxpayers. The "increase taxes" group came mostly from 1) bureaucrats, 2) politicians and 3) client groups in the population that depend on government spending for their paychecks.

Interestingly enough, this triumvirate supporting increased taxes is probably larger than the producing, working people that they expect to pay the taxes. In a democratic sense this is very scary, because now there is no limit on the taxes that you will pay. The group with the majority of the votes has a vested interest in more, not less, federal government spending.

So the Cut Spending First phenomenon was a nationwide, grass-roots taxpayer-fueled movement—a prairie fire of resentment—insisting that Congress and the President start solving the budget issue by starting to Cut Spending First. Talk show hosts from around the country picked it up, starting with Paul Harvey. Cut Spending First resulted in the most mail ever received by the White House or Congress—ever.

When I heard Paul Harvey on KSDO first say, "Cut Spending First," I brought it up on my show and endorsed the notion that it's time for taxpayers to be heard. The owner of Sorrento Mesa Printing heard me and called up.

"If I want to be in business ten years from now, this can't continue. It's not going to work, " he said.

"That's right," I said.

"Look," he continued, "I will print, for anyone who wants them, free cards addressed to each Congressman."

A few days later, a Postal Annex Plus manager called up and said, "We'll mail them for free." Soon, every Postal Annex Plus in the county, except one, provided free postage.

Then Rubio's owner said, "We'll distribute them. We'll have them at every Rubio's."

All the KSDO advertisers started jumping in, which was interesting because here was small business trying to assist grass roots taxpayers to resist big government.

And what started out in the early days of the Clinton White House as a debate on which taxes to increase quickly evolved into a debate about what could be cut. Politicians were falling over themselves everyday trying to propose new cuts in spending. "Here's my list," said every member of Congress, posturing to avoid being tagged as a "tax and spend" politician which, of course, all of them are. Every one of them. Republicans and Democrats alike have voted for the budgets over the last 25 years which have resulted in this debt crisis.

Ross Perot capitalized on that fact and got the largest third-party Presidential vote count ever. He continued to wage that war ever after the election. When the Clinton budget came out it did not attack entitlements, which is the largest and fastest growing part of the runaway spending, although progress was made on cutting back overhead, cutting back the Pentagon and progress was made in cutting total, overall spending.

But in addition, massive new taxes were enacted to help stem the red ink flood. Even so, under Clinton's best projections, not only will the deficit continue at about $200 billion a year (adding another $1 trillion of debt by 1997 to the $4 trillion we have now) the 1997 deficit is actually going to go up.

In other words, there has been no solution to the budget crisis but simply a feel-good, temporary postponement of the fact that we should be getting more serious about it. It will hit the fan in a big way in the coming years because you can't add health care to the mix without an explosion. The middle class, by 1997, will look back ten years and find that their standard of living has fallen, their taxes have doubled, their health care costs have gone up and the health care quality has gone down.

And of all the things the politicians promised, the exact opposite will happen. Clinton said, "No middle-class tax increase," and of course the middle class got a tax increase, with many more to come. Clinton said we would clean up health care by increasing the quality and lowering the cost for people. Exactly the opposite will happen. He said the deficit would go down. Exactly the opposite will happen. The debt will continue to rise and the proposition of the federal budget that has to go toward paying the interest on that debt will start to cripple vital government services.

Congress has already looted the Social Security System of its surplus. They've looted airport construction funds, highway construction funds, and every single program that is set aside for infrastructure to pay off the debt and pay off the entitlements, which are the critical parts of the deficit.

A New Coalition

Just as the Cut Spending First campaign brought together small business owners and middle-class taxpayers in a united, effective effort against the budget, I think that this partnership is the coalition of the future. It is the only coalition that can defeat the voracious appetite of big government and the tyranny that we are describing is the average, working producing taxpayer and the small businessman. The corporate people are just waiting to get on welfare.

Corporate Welfare

The big three auto makers just got on public welfare last year. Clinton went to them and said, OK, I'll do you a deal. I'll take over your R & D and we'll produce a car by 1998 that will get 50 miles to the gallon. Forget about antitrust rules, you guys get together because we've got to beat the foreign competition. The Undersecretary of State will be your liaison to me. Now, go to it.

So, they have now become welfare dependents. Their jobs are infinitely easier. They don't have to compete. They can collude on prices. They don't have to worry about someone coming out with a surprise car that will get too far ahead of the pack like the mini-vans did. Auto makers now have Big Brother to guarantee that they will stay in business.

They breathed a collective sigh of relief, went back to their offices and knocked off their two-martini lunch.

Dealing With It

But small business still has to deal with the real work in the marketplace. Small business has to deal with government bureaucracy, over-regulation and taxation as an overhead that hurts them in competing for your consumer dollar. So, the alliance of the small businesses and taxpayers is natural to try and stop this rip-off. Cut Spending First was the first step. Thousands of the postcards came from San Diego and hundreds of thousands poured into Congress.

In fact, freshman Congresswoman Lynn Schenk, who had just gotten to Washington, D.C., couldn't take the heat. She turned off her fax machine. We can't use it, said her staff, because it is continually bringing in messages.

In effect, Schenk was communicating this: We're not interested in hearing from our constituents.

Later she said it was because there were offensive messages and she named my show as a source. I challenged her to show me documentation.

"Was it offensive that we asked you to cut spending first, or was it offensive in some other way?" I asked in an interview.

She said, "No, it was personally offensive."

So I asked to see any personally offensive communications that she had received because of my show.

Shenk sent me one letter that she received, which was signed by a constituent, not sent anonymously.

"Dear Lynn, you incredible asshole," it began and then went on to describe what was wrong, as he saw it, with her representation in Congress. She found that offensive.

Now, it may not have been the choicest word that anyone would use to address a congress member, but that person signed their name. That's how they felt. Lynn better get used to it.

People are mad. People and taxpayers and small business people are threatened in their very existence by a tidal wave of bureaucrats, politicians and wards of the state—this growing welfare class from the General Motors chairman on down to the General Relief program— who all believe that their future is tied to a government relief program handout and a government regulation. And the rest of us who prop up that system with our taxpaying dollars are getting damn sick and tired of it.

Cut Spending First was the beginning of direct, public outcry to representatives on a massive scale. It was the beginning of the coalition between consumers and small business to demand a government that must balance its checkbook and tighten its belt, just like they must. And the campaign succeeded to change the attitude of elected officials from the President on down.

The subtext of the Cut Spending First card read, "I'll be watching." For this to be a truly effective political tool, we must watch and we must act upon what we see. That part is up to us.

Chapter Ten

You Get What You Deserve

*Somewhere deep down
we know that in the final analysis
we do decide things and that even our decisions
to let someone else decide
are really our decisions, however pusillanimous.*
—Harvey G. Cox, 1967

The oldest cliche in democracy is, "If you don't vote, don't complain." But the truth is, both people who vote and people who don't vote have no idea of the power of a single vote. With fewer and fewer turning out to vote, each vote now counts more than ever.

Without going through all the numerous examples of elections that were decided by a handful of votes, the truth is that low turnouts have meant that determined minorities have turned elections around.

For instance, on the issue of abortion, determined activists have elected and "un-elected" hosts of officials at the local, state and federal levels over the last 20 years. And the lower the turnout, the more likely the success of these advocates, to the detriment of the broad range of issues that comes before any elected official.

It's In The Stats

Lets look more closely at the voting pattern in San Diego County. According to records from the San Diego County Registrar of Voters, Conny McCormack, in the years between 1980 and 1990, the percentage of those registered to vote in San Diego County that actually did vote went from 53.1 percent down to 36.5 percent. The population rose by about 250,000.

The primary elections show even a more dismal downturn. In 1980 39.2 percent of all those eligible to vote cast ballots. By 1990 that had dropped to 23.9 percent. This is more significant when you realize that it is usually the primary election that ousts an incumbent and causes a shake-up.

Statistically, we can also see a surge of interest in the 1992 elections. DRIP — Don't Reelect Incumbent Politicians — made its impact felt as the primary election voters suddenly jumped from 23.9 percent to 28.8 percent. In the general election, the percentage of the people casting ballots jumped up nearly to 1984 levels at 51.2 percent. In other words, each vote is twice as powerful.

It Doesn't Take Much

As a result, it doesn't take many votes to turn the tide of an election. For instance, in the 1992 primary elections, the adult population of San Diego County eligible to vote was 1,959,000. Registered voters stood at 1,254,269. A whopping 704,731 adults didn't even register to vote! But even more disappointing, only 564,394,or 28.8 percent of all eligible adults voted.

Since the primary elections usually have a number of candidates in the running, the number of voters making the difference is amazingly small. In the 49th Congressional District General Election of 1992, with 248,894 adults voting in that district, Lynn Schenk won with 51.14 percent of the vote, while her opponent, Judy Jarvis, had only 20,000 fewer votes. That's less than half the student population of San Diego State University.

You Gotta Register

Voter registration forms are available at post offices, libraries, from clerks at city and county offices, at chamber of commerce offices and at the Department of Motor Vehicles (remember the motor/voter bill???). You can also call the San Diego County Registrar of Voters office at 570-1061 to find other locations or to get forms mailed to you..

Your registration card must be mailed in 29 days prior to the date of the next election to be eligible to vote. To register legally, you must be a citizen of the United States, a resident of California, be at least 18 years of age by the date of the next election, be mentally competent and not in prison or on parole for the conviction of a felony. If you meet these qualifications you can vote. You must re-register if you move, change your name or change your political party affiliation. You can even vote if you're homeless and living on the street. In that case the card just asks for cross streets.

Get Out The Vote

Registering to vote is one of those things that people keep meaning to do but don't do until it's put right in front of them. Registering others to vote may be one of the most significant acts of protest that you can undertake. It's not hard. You can get batches of Voter Registration Cards and detailed instructions from the Registrar of Voters office at 5201 Ruffin Road, Suite I in San Diego. Caesar Clark Bolchini, a registration services workers, has just completed a new, simplified flip chart that tells you exactly what to do and anticipates most of your questions about the process.

Seize The Initiative, Referendum And Recall

These three mechanisms from the Progressive Era in the early 20th Century, are available at all levels of California government. They are not available at the federal level. That's an important difference in the way our democracy works in this state. Every legal subdivision in California, from the Governor down to water districts, is subject to initiative, referendum and recall.

The best source for information about getting a measure on a ballot is the Registrar of Voters office. Several publications are available there to explain all of the specific petition requirements will be explained to you.

In general, here's how initiative, referendum and recall works:

INITIATIVE — California citizens can write their own legislation for any level of government in California by getting the required number of signatures. (It varies from 5 to 15 percent of the number of people who voted in the last election.) Initiative measures can be put on the ballot to change anything from the way that the water district does its billing (why not more disclosure of the actual cost of the water, hmmmm?) to, as in Proposition 174, the way we finance education throughout the state.

A booklet called "California Ballot Initiatives" available free from the Registrar of Voters briefly summarizes the initiative process in 12 pages. It gives the names and addresses of various state officials, citations to the Elections Code and the approximate dates for completion of the numerous steps to be completed.

REFERENDUM - Using the referendum, citizens can react to ordinances or legislation already passed by any level of California government, from the water district through the city and county to the state legislature. Again, if you have a certain number of signatures of voters, you can force a special election or put the measure on a scheduled ballot to allow all the voters to decide whether that legislation should stay or go.

Once the people have voted, initiatve and referendum become law, without any veto or political trade-offs or amendment of any kind. This is direct democracy. At the state level, the initiative goes into law as soon as the Secretary of State certifies that it received a majority vote. A referendum or initiative cannot be undone, unless a court finds it unconstitutional or the voters in a subsequent election vote to repeal or amend it.

RECALL - Finally, if you don't like the legislator, you can actually kick out of office any elected official before his or her term of office expires. This is, again, a petition process requiring a number of signatures usually based on a certain percentage of the total vote in the last election.

These three avenues of direct participation to keep the heat on elected officials are available all the way down from the state legislature to the lighting, fire or water districts — every political division in the state of California is subject to those three processes. Don't say there is nothing you can do. You have a right of direct participation that is actually very easy. All you need are people that agree with you.

The Way We Do Things Around Here

At the local level, in the City of San Diego, there is a variation on this process. If you come before the City Council with a referendum (in other words, if you don't like something they've passed and you actually come in with the signatures to change it) the City Council has a given period of time to repeal what they did in order to avoid having it go to a public vote.

Similarly, if someone comes in with an initiative petition and the signatures, the City Council has the chance to pass it as a law and not have to go to the voters at all.

For example, the construction of several high rise buildings along our coast in San Diego inspired a 1972 initative calling for a 30-ft. height limit on buildings. This passed and has saved San Diego from the Miami-ization of our shoreline.

Sometimes you don't even need the signatures. Just the threat of referendum, for example, on the parking fee issue was the major reason that the city council reversed itself. If there had been no referendum, no way for the city voters to have actually overruled the city council, the council would probably have gone ahead with the fees. Instead, the majority did an about face and rejected the parking fees. They knew how very easily those outraged citizens could get enough signatures and force the issue to be put on the next ballot and they would look like idiots. That's why they turned around.

These citizen procedures are definitely mechanisms to get accountability out of elected officials. Its important for people to know how easy it is to do.

Good News, Bad News

One of the reasons that these petitions have become more powerful is because their success is often tied to the percentage of voters who voted in the last election. When that number of voters that show up at the polls goes down, the ability to act directly goes up. The job is half what it used to be to implement direct democracy because only half the people are registered and even fewer vote. It's the good news/bad news.

For instance, in the County of San Diego the formula is based on the 672,522 voters who cast ballots in the General Election of 1990. That number stays effective until November of 1994 when the next election for Governor is held. A petition with 20 percent of the voters, 134,522, will cause a special election to be held, but only 10 percent are needed to have a measure on the next regular ballot. That's 67,253 signatures.

For the City of San Diego, the figures are based on the number of registered voters (642,355). An initiative would take 10 percent, (64,236), but a referendum requires only 5 percent, (32,118). That's a little less than how many people work within walking distance of Horton Plaza. It's an effort that would take planning and organization, but it definitely can be done.

But if you are from Del Mar the process might be even easier. The signatures required on these petitions are based on the total number of registered voters, which, as of Oct. 1, 1993 was still only 3,974. Initiatives and referendums go on the ballot with only 10 percent, or 396 signatures. You can call for a special election in Del Mar with only 594 names. That's the good news.

The bad news is that determined, active minorities can put all kinds of crazy stuff on the ballot and the voters are going to have to deal with it. We have had some elections where there were dozens of initiatives, statewide and local, on the ballot.

Would You Like To Sign?

Petition signatures are the most costly and time-consuming part of qualifying an initiative or referendum for the ballot. Only persons who are registered, qualified voters are entitled to sign. Each person may only sign an initiative petition once or all their signatures become invalid. People circulating petitions must also be registered voters and are responsible for following various rules about making false statements about the petition, including whether the petitioner is volunteering or being paid.

Signatures are verified by the Registrar of Voters office by random sampling. If the number of signatures in the sample is less than 95 percent valid, the petition does not qualify. If the number of valid signatures is greater than 110 percent of the requirement, the petition is qualified without further verification. If the number of signatures is between 95 and 110 percent, the registrars examine each and every signature.

All in all, it may be surprisingly easy to force change in the laws by putting your own legislation before the voters. It has certainly been done before. The whole tax revolt of Proposition 13, the school choice initiative, auto insurance and dozens of other examples at the state and local levels exist to show that there have been major shifts in public policies led not by elected officials but by direct intervention by the voters. Ultimately, we have no one to blame for bad government here in California but ourselves.

Chapter Eleven

Courting Disaster

*Because just as good morals, if they are to be maintained,
have need of the laws, so the laws, if they are to be observed,
have need of good morals.*
—Niccolo Machiavelli, 1965

The absolute last resort for citizens seeking redress is the court system. It's cumbersome, archaic, inexplicable and expensive. But for many people it is a way to fight a system that is otherwise closed to their input or violating the constitution as these citizens see it.

Legal processes are available to individuals to challenge the actions of government or to command the actions of government. Some of these processes go back to the Middle Ages in English common law. For instance, the right of an English citizen to compel a king to justice goes back 600 years. That action is called a "Mandamus", a Latin word which requests that the court compel the government to do the right thing.

In addition, American courts have the right to determine whether or not the actions of the legislature are constitutional. Since they interpret what the constitution means, the courts are a constant check upon the laws passed by legislation or initiative or referendum.

When It All Got Started

The court system, in the beginning of our republic, was never meant to be a place where citizens would find redress of grievances against government. The Congress was supposed to be that place. The Congress, for example, would ideally thrash through the abortion issue and come out with a democratic consensus expressed as legislation. Instead, that bitter and dangerous-to-re-election issue was left to the Supreme Court in Roe vs. Wade. And everybody in the system knows it was a cop-out. It is not the way the system is supposed to work.

Over the past several decades liberals have used the court systems very effectively for civil rights issues, environmental issues and labor issues. Again, this has been done because of the perceived failure of the legislature to take their demands into account and use the legislative process in the way the Founding Fathers intended.

Two Can Play That Game

Lately, the conservative right wing has come to understand that the court process can be used to achieve their political goals as well. Conservative counterparts to the ACLU, such as the Center for Law and Justice, the Pacific Legal Foundation and the Individual Rights Foundation have used suits to reinforce property rights, to defeat affirmative action quota systems and to reassert land development rights against outrageously drawn environmental rules.

So the court system has become a parallel to the legislative process where different factions have brought their unresolved issues and fought each other.

Do The Right Thing

In today's law, there is an action called an Administrative Mandamus. It can be filed by any citizen to compel any agency to live up to its own laws and rules. These actions have been brought fairly frequently to compel agencies to act. For example, a citizen may file the action to compel the city to issue a building permit when it has not been following its own procedure. This type of action is not punitive and does not go after money. It's a way to get action.

It's Unconstitutional

There is another kind of lawsuit that asks the court to declare that actions of government unconstitutional. This is the type of suit used to remove the crosses and the nativity scenes from public land.

If you can fund the enormous cost of attorneys and the time — this is the most time-consuming way to go about making a change in government — these lawsuits do change government behavior.

For instance, it was an individual parent in the San Diego Unified School District who sued back in the '60s to compel the district to begin a bussing program to achieve racial integration. This year alone that lawsuit cost the San Diego Unified School District over $14 million dollars. It takes that money directly out of educational quality and puts it directly into the notion that by moving some students around you can increase test scores.

Despite the fact that bussing has now been proven to have no improving affect on test scores, the courts still require it. So one individual, using the court system to review the actions of government, can change those actions or can even require actions to be taken, even though they cost millions and millions of dollars and totally skew the rest of the democratic process.

A Half A Cent Is Better Than None

Dick Rider's lawsuit centered on whether or not the County's Proposition A of 1990, which purported to grant a new agency taxation rights for law enforcement purposes, violated Proposition 13. Proposition 13, put in the California Constitution a 2/3 majority vote requirement to approve any new tax. Proposition A in 1990 added the 1/2 cent sales tax with a simple majority vote and began collecting it. Was this unconstitutional? Did this vote violate Proposition 13? The Superior Court said, "Yes", the Appeals Court said "No" and the California Supreme Court said, "Yes."

This suit was brought by a coalition of committed people who felt that the government was violating the constitution. Formed with the name United Taxpayers (UN-TAX), the grassroots effort battled opponents who had spent $250,000 on advertising to get Prop. A passed in the first place. Their opponents had spoken throughout the county at 400 different meetings and had the support of the Copley press and all of the television stations.

But they went to the court and went all the way.

We Can't Give It Back

Following the successful court action to repeal this 1/2-cent sales tax, there was a classic example of how the "Imperial Bureaucracy" doesn't care much about the constitution when it works against them. The courts ruled that the tax was illegally collected by government, it was unconstitutionally collected and they had no authority to collect it. But meanwhile the county had already collected over $300 million while the lawsuit worked its way through the courts. The question was, what do they do with the money that they have no right to have? The answer was, "We ain't giving it back."

The State Board of Equalization said, "We collected it and it was valid until the court said it wasn't, so we're going to keep all the money." Dick Rider's group had to go back into court and the court had to rule that when they ruled the tax unconstitutional, they meant it was unconstitutional from day one. And because it was, the government had to give all the money back.

But even then the bureaucrats wouldn't. Instead, they went to the legislature and said, "You're going to have to give us a process. We have no way of giving money back that we've collected illegally, so we're not going to do it. You tell us how."

In the meantime they were still collecting the money.

The court had to order the government to stop collecting the tax! Then everyone had all kinds of ideas for getting rid of it. "Let's give it to the counties for law enforcement, anyway," they said.

Finally there was so much public outcry that Senator Lucy Killea carried legislation to reduce the San Diego sales tax by 1/2 cent until the over-collection was offset by under-collection. This would more or less return it to the same people. Those who spent $5,000 or more on a special purchase could make a special claim. That got support and passed. The reduced sales tax was to start in April of 1994. But the San Diego Superior Court Juedge Lawrence Kapiloff issued an order with yet another scheme for returning the money!

To this day, three years later, we still have not seen the money. So, it is interesting to note that even if you win in court, the bureaucratic tyranny that is growing at every level of government says, "So What?"

A Grand Idea

There is another way for citizens to address complaints about the functions of government and that is by taking them to the Grand Jury. In California, the Grand Jury in every county is mandated to indict individuals for criminal activities. They also have a very strong civil oversight responsibility in terms of the functioning of local government.

Remember the Jim Wade case with Child Protective Services? He was accused of raping his 4-year-old daughter, even though she described an assailant who came in the window. Over a year later, after she had been removed from the home and the family destroyed, police reviewed the evidence and discovered that forensic evidence they had had from the first day proved the father was not the assailant. And they had in custody a rapist from the same apartment complex whose M.O. was going through windows.

Information about this case was given to the county Grand Jury that led to a total investigation of Child Protective Services to see if it had a balanced approach between child protection and family integrity.

Similarly, Dave Sossaman took information on welfare fraud to the county Grand Jury which started a year-long investigation. This resulted in a tremendous documentation of fraud that would never have seen the light of day otherwise.

In addition to the County Grand Jury, there is a Federal Grand Jury in San Diego, but its review action is much more limited. The Federal Grand Jury focuses on issues such as drug smuggling, illegal aliens and corruption of government officials. Both of these Grand Juries are composed of everyday San Diego citizens.

How do you get on the County Grand Jury? Jurors are nominated by a judge, then are appointed by the Presiding Judge to one-year terms. Once you are seated on the Grand Jury, you review requests for investigations and set your agenda for the year.

Ladies And Gentlemen Of The Jury

According to the rulings of the United States courts, the trial jury in any legal case, civil or criminal, has an independent right to its opinion. Even though the jury is guided by the evidence and the direction of the judge, the determination of what is just is up to the jury. Nobody can tell them they don't have a right to make up their own mind. There is one instruction given by the judge that says, basically, You have the right to make up your own mind. Every judge has to admit, when all is said and done, it's up to the jury.

Know Your Rights

Jim Harnsburger is interested in educating people who serve on juries about this very fact. He feels juries are often manipulated and intimidated. Instructions claim, "You have to do that, here's what you have to listen to, forget what you think is true." Harnsburger says, "That's not right." And apparently there are lots of other people who agree with him in an organization called the Fully Informed Jury Association.

Locally, Harnsburger has formed a group known as the Citizens Rule Book Committee. The committee distributes a handbook that clearly spells out to jurors that they have the right to decide their own mind and vote their conscience in every case. And he passes out this handbook on the steps of the courts.

"It started when a friend of mine was serving on a jury and he wanted to be educated about how to fight bad laws," said Harnsburger. "I gave him and handbook and he took it into the jury room.

"Well, the judge and the marshal confiscated the book, threw him off the jury and called it 'tampering.' This made me so mad that I went down to the court and started passing out the books to jurors myself.

"Now I have five court orders against me. Two marshals came up to me on the steps of the San Diego courthouse and threatened me with arrest. I told them to go ahead. 'I'll take this into the courts and I'll insist on a jury trial,' I said. They just walked away."

Jim Harnsburger's insistence on the power of jurors found a perfect test case in the public disturbance over the Jaime Guzman case. On October 23, 1993, Jaime Guzman, a young family man from San Ysidro, was asleep in his apartment one evening. He heard noises outside and heard a truck start up and realized that it was the sound of his own truck being stolen.

Guzman lives in an area that is plagued by car theft as each and every night hundreds of illegal immigrants cross the border and sweep the border neighborhoods for anything they can get their hands on to steal and sell. In this particular case, some young illegal Mexicans were stealing his car to transport more aliens north.

Quickly, Guzman grabbed his gun and ran down to the parking lot. He got there as the car, which represented his livelihood, was racing down the street. Guzman fired some shots at the thieves and the passenger was hit.

Who was arrested? Jaime Guzman. The illegals who stole his car ran away. The passenger who was shot was taken to the hospital, treated with your money and is living in Los Angeles at your expense.

My listeners and I at KSDO were furious. The victim was arrested and the criminals went free. Now here was a case where it would be vital for jurors to know that they have the right to vote their conscience. Harnsburger organized a protest of 100 people to stand outside the courtroom at Guzman's arraignment and made it clear to all the media that whatever the District Attorney may think and whatever the judge may instruct and whatever courtroom antics were used to twist the truth, the jury had the ultimate power to wield justice for Jaime Guzman.

Guzman ultimatly entered into a plea bargain to avoid a trial, a tactic often employed by the District Attorney to get the conviction while avoiding a jury.

Courtroom Drama - Can You Have An Effect?

In the past 50 years, San Diego has had only two District Attorneys. The current District Attorney has served for 23 years and plans to run for reelection. On his staff are no less than 45 Deputy District Attorneys, all making over $85,000 per year and working in one of the most luxurious office buildings in San Diego. And at the top of the building, in an enormous office overlooking San Diego bay, sits District Attorney Ed Miller.

A few blocks away, Dale Akiki, a multiple-handicapped individual, has spent 2 1/2 years in a tiny cell before even coming to trial on 52 counts of child abuse. During an incredible trial which took most of 1993 - one of the longest and most expensive trial in the history of the county - citizens on both side of this emotionally-charged issue have jumped in to try to influence the workings of the criminal justice process as it related to this case.

Dale Akiki, his wife and another woman were teaching the children at Faith Chapel in Spring Valley while the kids' parents attended a 90-minute church service. Four months after leaving this post, one child, at the end of a full day of questioning by her mother made one comment that suggested inappropriate behavior. This suggestion was a spark that inflamed imagination of this charismatic, "devil-in-every-corner" congregation and flamed into hysteria.

One very active church member had been involved in learning about Satanic ritual abuse of children. This perspective swept through the congregation and fanned the flame into accounts of by children of baby stabbings, sexual games, kidnapping, wild animals in the classroom and death threats by Akiki.

The original deputy district attorney assigned to the case came to the conclusion that there was insufficient evidence and it was not a prosecutable case. The witnesses, including the very young children involved, were not reliable. There was no circumstantial evidence, no physical evidence and no forensic evidence that any of these activities ever took place at all.

A respected individual who heads the Foodmaker Corporation approached District Attorney Ed Miller, at the urging of his wife. Jack Goodall was concerned that the prosecution move forward, in spite of the recommendation of the deputy district attorney that it not.

Mr. Goodall's position was that there was evidence of ritual abuse and he wanted a prosecution. He presented his case in person to the District Attorney — a very, very unusual meeting. Ed Miller does not usually listen to anyone from the outside when he decides whether or not to prosecute a case. He's a stubborn individual and, to his credit, he has generally kept away from being influence by buddies or passing out favors. In this case, in this meeting, which no one has denied took place, Ed Miller listened to a personal plea from Jack Goodall. Why?

This was more than a courtesy meeting. Deputy District Attorney Mary Avery was assigned the case. Avery is a founding member of the Child Abuse Prevention Foundation. District Attorney Ed Miller, Mary Avery and Jack and Mary Goodall all sit on the board of directors of the Child Abuse Prevention Foundation. Mary Avery and Mary Goodall served together on the Ritual Abuse Task Force for San Diego County, now disbanded.

Why Would They Lie?

The crux of the witness approach in this case is identical to the now-famous McMartin Preschool trial and other cases that are coming to light across the United States. Psychologists, in a series of sessions lasting, in some cases, over months and years, questioned children until the answers fit pre-conceived suspicions of child abuse. In the Akiki case, many of the therapists questioning the children had received training in Satanic ritual abuse as well.

During the trial, Avery used those children's testimony which fit most closely with the pre-conceived notions of abuse, and did not use the testimony, including the questionings of the first child to make an accusation of abuse, that supported acquittal. The childrens' accusations were clearly inconsistent and contradictory over time.

Recent scientific studies, as reported by John Stossel on ABC's newsprogram "20/20" last October indicate that this type of testimony is almost always made up. Researchers took a control group of children and asked them the following question once each week on video tape, "Do you remember when you got your finger caught in the mousetrap?"

The first week, the child dismissed the question entirely. The second time, the child said, "No, I don't think so." The third time his answer was more elaborate and by the eleventh time the child has made up a whole story. He talked about how he went down to the basement and the mousetrap was hidden by the woodpile and his dad asked him to get firewood and he stuck his finger in and the mousetrap went off and he had an owie and he had to go to the doctor.

There was a long, made-up story because the child thought, This guy is asking the question over and over and wants to hear something. So Stossel showed video tapes of children who are trying to get the questioning adults to approve of them and go away and leave them alone. They would say anything to make it happen.

Then Stossel showed more serious video tapes of a child psychologist asking a child who was a "witness" to abuse, "What happened when Rev. So and So did this..." and he grabbed the child from behind and made as if to thrust into him. It made me fall out of my chair. It was clear how children can be manipulated by therapy.

The children are ultimately the victims because they think these horrible things actually happened to them.

Trial and Error

Dale Akiki's case went forward. Rose Marie Royster, a housewife, heard about this case like everyone else in San Diego. It bothered her. You mean, she thought, this guy from the church, because he has some kind of credibility with Ed Miller is able to turn around the prosecution, keep this man in jail for 2 1/2 years with no conviction, serving time as a handicapped man, because they think some satanic ritual abuse went on of which there is absolutely no evidence? So she became involved.

The more she learned, the more she disliked.

She started talking to the community and to her friends and found that there were a lot of others who felt the same way. Pretty soon there was a support group for Dale Akiki. Pretty soon there were are demonstrations, fund-raisers, press conferences, press releases and all kinds of mobilization of the community against this prosecution. At this printing, the trial continues.

You Can Influence A Judge, Too

The point is, the criminal justice and court systems are not objective, above-the-fray, always-dignified processes. Taking place in the courtroom is a political process in which powerful people are trying to get justice for their own aims. And not-so-powerful people are trying to do the same thing. And you should too.

Because I'm not just talking about the planning department, the zoning codes, the city and the Congressmen — all the things that we know are political and subject to pressure. I want you to know that you can participate in the court system — through jury duty or protests or law suits — to make the system work for YOU. If you don't cry for justice, you surely won't get it.

Conclusion

Organize,
Act,
WIN!

In order to act, you must be somewhat insane.
A reasonably sensible man is satisfied with thinking.
—George Clemenceau

If you are defending your constitutional rights, or taking an action to enhance your community or simply trying to stop the latest outrage by some government agency, I hope the stories of your fellow San Diegans contained in this book will inspire you to organize, act and win. To "Fight City Hall" and WIN!

These stories are but a representative sampling of the many heroes who daily, among San Diego's citizens, seek to create a better life and future for themselves, their families and those around them through direct participation in our society. It is a paradox of our time that the American system that was originally set up to encourage and promote this participation, has now deteriorated to the point where participation is often discouraged and sometimes even punished.

This book seeks not only to inspire your participation despite difficulties and obstacles. Through the stories I've told, I hope I've indicated how to translate your concerns, goals and frustrations into effective, winning action. Each individual case is just that—individual and unique. Your tactics to organize, act and win might be very different than those you have read about in this book. I encourage you, first of all, to decide to act and then to share that decision with me on the air at KSDO.

The purpose of my Community Forum on KSDO is to allow people like you to break through the media barrier and mobilize others who agree with your concern or goal or frustration to act. Because the truth is, your individual decision to act may not win unless you mobilize your fellow citizens to act with you.

Those of you who believe that government will secure your rights, and that there's no need to fight for them; that government will protect your interests and there's no reason to organize to protect your own interests; that government will act in the "public interest" and there's no need for the individual to bother, are not only sadly mistaken but in the coming few years are likely to pay a huge price for your apathy and indifference.

Today's problems in America are growing exponentially along with the power of government to deter public participation, promote an "Imperial Bureaucracy" and convert your God-given rights into government entitlements. The need for your activism to counterbalance the caterwauling of the left is more critical today than ever.

The difference that elevates ordinary people to the status of heroes is simply this: some people encountering evil can walk away and leave it to someone else. Others, such as those you have met in the pages of this book, when they meet evil must act to resist it.

Which side are you on?

Appendix

Where To Write, Who To Call

Table of Contents

General Information

REGISTRAR OF VOTERS
5201 Ruffin Road, Suite I
PO Box 85093
San Diego, CA 92186-5093
General Information
(619) 570-1061
Absentee/Mail Ballot Voting
(619) 570-1064
PO Box 85520
San Diego, CA 92186-5520
Campaign Disclosure
(619) 694-3407
Candidate Filing
(619) 694-3405
Precinct Planning *(Maps)*
(619) 694-3199
Telecommunications Device for the Deaf (TDD)
(619) 694-3441/FAX (619) 694-2955

SECRETARY OF STATE
1230 J Street
Sacramento, CA 95814-2907
General Information
(916) 445-6371
Election Information
(916) 445-0820
Political Reform Division
(Campaign Finances)
(916) 322-4880
Telecommunications Device for the Deaf (TDD)
(800) 833-8683
Voter Registration Forms
(24 Hours in English)
(800) 345-VOTE
Voter Registration Forms
(24 Hours in Spanish)
(800) 345-VOTA
Fair Political Practices Commission (FPPC)
428 J Street, Suite 700
PO Box 807
Sacramento, CA 95804-0807

Technical Assistance
(916) 322-5662
Federal Election Commission (FEC)
999 E Street, NW
Washington, DC 20463-0001
Campaign Finances for Federal Offices
(800) 424-9530
Capitol Switchboard
United States Senate or Members of Congress (not listed in this directory)
(202) 224-3121
Federal Information Center
General Information
(800) 726-4995
League of Women Voters
General Information
(619) 298-0032

Government Clerks

San Diego County Clerk
Annette Evans - 237-0502
(recorded information 531-5246
FAX 557-4155

CITY CLERKS

Chula Vista
Beverly Authelet - 691-5041
Coronado
Jacqueline Wilson - 522-7320
Del Mar
Patti Barnes - 755-9313
El Cajon
Marilynn Linn - 441-1761
FAX 441-1537
Imperial Beach
Cynthia Tjarks - 423-8300
La Mesa
Anita Underwood - 463-6611
Lemon Grove
Christine Taub - 464-6934
National City
Lori Anne Peoples - 336-4226

Poway
Marjorie Wahlsten - 679-4237
San Diego
Charles Abdelnour - 533-4000
FAX 533-4045
Santee
Loretta Roper - 258-4100
Solana Beach
Deborah Harrington - 755-2998
Carlsbad
Aletha Rautenkraz - 434-2808
Encinitas
Jane Pool - 633-2600
Escondido
Joanne Bunch - 741-4616
Oceanside
Barbara Riegel Wayne - 966-4460
San Marcos
Sheila Kennedy - 744-4020
Vista
Joe Siebert - 726-1340 x3256

Public Officials

FEDERAL OFFICES

President
Bill Clinton (D)—1992-1996
The White House
1600 Pennsylvania Avenue
Washington, DC 20500
(202) 456-1414
FAX (202) 456-2461
Vice President
Al Gore (D)—1992-1996

United States Senate
Diane Feinstein (D)—1992-1994
Washington Address
331 Hart Senate Office Bldg.
Washington, DC 20510-0004
(202) 224-3841
District Address
750 B Street, #3030
San Diego, CA 92101-9712

Barbara Boxer (D)
Washington Address
112 Hart Senate Office Bldg.
Washington, DC 20510-0004
(202) 224-3553
District Address
2250 East Imperial Highway, #545
El Segundo, CA 90245-3546
(310) 414-5700

Representative In Congress
Capitol Switch Board (202) 224-3121
*(To contact a Member of Congress or
United States Senate not listed in this
directory.)*

48th District
Ron Packard (R)—1992-1994
2162 Rayburn House Office Bldg.
Washington, DC 20515-0548
(202) 225-3906
District Address
221 East Vista Way, #205
Vista, CA 92084-6009
(619) 631-1364

49th District
Lynn Schenk (D)—1992-1994
315 Cannon House Office Bldg.
Washington, DC 20515-0552
(202) 225-2040
District Address
3900 Fifth Avenue, #200
San Diego, CA 92130-3112
(619) 291-1430

50th District
Bob Filner (D)—1992-1994
504 Cannon House Office Bldg.
Washington, DC 20515-0552
(202) 225-8045
District Address
333 F Street, #A
Chula Vista, CA 91910-2624
(619) 422-5963

51st District
Randy "Duke" Cunningham (R)
—1992-1994
117 Cannon House Office Bldg.
Washington, DC 20515-0552
(202) 225-5452
District Address
613 West Valley Parkway, #320
Escondido, CA 92025-2549
(619) 737-8438

52nd District
Duncan Hunter (R)—1992-1994
133 Cannon House Office Bldg.
Washington, DC 20515-0552
(202) 225-5672
District Address
366 South Pierce Street
El Cajon, CA 92020-4136
(619) 579-3001

STATE OFFICES

Governor
Pete Wilson (R)—1990-1994
State Capitol
Sacramento, CA 95814-4905
(916) 445-2841
FAX (916) 445-4633
District Address
1350 Front Street, #6054
San Diego, CA 92101-3614
(619) 525-4640

Lieutenant Governor
Leo McCarthy (D)—1990-1994
State Capitol, Rm. 1114
Sacramento, CA 95814-4905
(916) 445-8994
District Address
5777 West Century, #1650
Los Angeles, CA 90045-7402
(310) 412-6118

Secretary of State
March Fong (D)—1990-1994
1230 J Street
Sacramento, CA 95814-2907
General Information (916) 445-6371
Election Information (916) 445-0820
FAX (916) 324-4573

Controller
Gray Davis (D)—1990-1994
300 Capitol Mall, 18th Floor
Sacramento, CA 95814-4340
(916) 445-2636
District Address
1964 Westwood Boulevard, #310
Los Angeles, CA 90025-4651
(310)446-8846

Treasurer
Kathleen Brown (D)—1990-1994
915 Capitol Mall, Rm. 110
Sacramento, CA 95814-4810
(916) 653-2894
FAX (916) 653-3125
District Address
304 South Broadway, #500
Los Angeles, CA 90013-1209
(213) 620-5384

Attorney General
Daniel E. Lungren (R)—1990-1994
1515 K Street, Rm. 511
Sacramento, CA 95814-4017
(800) 952-5225 or
(916) 445-9555
District Address
300 Spring Street, #500
Los Angeles, CA 90013-1232
(213) 897-2000

Insurance Commissioner
John Garamendi (D)—1990-1994
One City Centre, Suite 1120
770 L Street

Sacramento, CA 95814-3313
(916) 445-5544
District Address
300 Spring Street, 14th Floor
Los Angeles, CA 90013-1233
(213) 346-6400

Board of Equalization - 3rd District
Ernest Dronenburg, Jr. (R)—1990-1994
450 N Street, MIC:77
Sacramento, CA 95814-5691
(916) 445-5713
FAX (916) 324-2586
District Address
110 West C Street, #1709
San Diego, CA 92101-3909
(619) 237-7844
FAX (619) 237-7229

Superintendent of Public Instruction
Vacant (*)
(Term expires in 1994)
California Department of Education
721 Capital Mall, Room 524
Sacramento, CA 95814-4702
(916) 657-5485
FAX (916) 657-5101

Chief Justice, Supreme Court
Malcolm Lucas (*) **
Supreme Court of California
303 Second Street
South Tower, 8th Floor
San Francisco, CA 94107-1366
(415) 396-9400

Nonpartisan Offices
**Appointed by Governor; confirmed by*
voters every 12 years.

STATE LEGISLATURE

California State Senate
36th District
Robert Presley (D)—1990-1994

State Capitol, Room 4048
Sacramento, CA 95814-4905
(916) 445-9781
District Address
3600 Lime Street, #111
Riverside, CA 92501-2972
(909) 782-4111

37th District
David G. Kelley (R)—1992-1996
State Capitol, Rm. 3082
Sacramento, CA 95814-4905
(916) 445-5581
District Address
11440 West Bernardo Court, #104
San Diego, CA 92127-1642
(619) 675-8211

38th District
William A. "Bill" Craven (R)
—1990-1994
State Capitol, Room 3070
Sacramento, CA 95814-4905
District Address
2121 Palomar Airport Road, #100
Carlsbad, CA 92009-1422
(619) 744-2223 / (619) 438-3814

39th District
Lucy Killea (I)—1992-1996
State Capitol, Rm. 4062
Sacramento, CA 95814-4905
(916) 445-3952
District Address
2550 Fifth Avenue, #152
San Diego, CA 92103-6622
(619) 696-8930
FAX (619) 696-8930

40th District
Wadie P. Deddeh (D)—1990-1994
State Capitol, Rm. 3048
Sacramento, CA 95814-4905
(916) 445-6767
District Address

430 Davidson Street, #C
Chula Vista, CA 91910-2494
(619) 427-7080

Member of the State Assembly
Mailing address for all
Assemblymembers: PO Box 942849,
Sacramento, CA 92000
249-0001

66th District
Ray Haynes (R)—1992-1994
State Capitol, Rm. 5119
Sacramento, CA 95814-4905
(916) 445-1676
District Address
29377 Rancho California Road
Temecula, CA 92591-5201
(90) 699-1113

73rd District
Bill Morrow (R)—1992-1994
State Capitol, Rm. 2111
Sacramento, CA 95814-4905
(916) 445-7676
FAX (916) 323-8318
District Address
PO Box 62
Oceanside, CA 92049-0062
302 North Hill Street
Oceanside, CA 92054-2824
(619) 434-9947

74th District
Robert Frazee (R)—1992-1994
State Capitol, Rm 6028
Sacramento, CA 95814
(916) 445-2390
FAX (916) 324-9991
District Address
2121 Palomar Airport Road, #105
Carlsbad, CA 92009-1422
(619) 438-5665
FAX (619) 438-6620

75th District
Jan Goldsmith (R)—1992-1994
State Capitol, Rm 2002
Sacramento, CA 95814-4905
(916) 445-2484
District Address
12307 Oak Knoll Drive, #A
Poway, CA 92064-5319
(619) 486-5191

76th District
Mike Gotch (D)—1992-1994
State Capitol, Rm 4146
Sacramento, CA 95814-4905
(916) 445-7210
District Address
1080 University Avenue, #H-201
San Diego, CA 92103-3363
(619) 294-7600

77th District
Tom Connolly (D)—1992-1994
State Capitol, Rm. 2170
Sacramento, CA 95814-4905
(916) 445-3266
3293 Olive Avenue
Lemon Grove, CA 91945-1723
(619) 465-7723

78th District
Deirdre "Dede" Alpert (D)—1992-1994
State Capitol, RM 3173
Sacramento, CA 95814-4905
(916) 445- 2112
District Address
1350 Front Street, #6013
San Diego, CA 92101-3614
(619) 234-7878
FAX (619) 233-0078

79th District
Steve Peace (D)—1992-1994
State Capitol, Rm 2184
Sacramento, CA 95814-4905
(916) 445-7556

FAX (916) 322-2271
District Address
430 Davidson Street, #B
Chula Vista, CA 91910-2494
(619) 426-1617
FAX (619) 696-5430

COUNTY OFFICES

Board of Supervisors

1st District
Brian Bilbray—1992-1996
County Administration Center
1600 Pacific Highway, #335
San Diego, CA 92101-2470
(619) 531-5511
District Address
430 Davicson Street, #D
Chula Vista, CA 91910-2411
(619) 691-4700

2nd District
Dianne Jacob—1992-1996
County Administration Center
1600 Pacific Highway, #335
San Diego, CA 92101-2470
(619) 531-5522
District Address
250 East Main Street, #I-69
El Cajon, CA 92020-3941
(619) 441-4327

3rd District
Pam Slater—1992-1996
County Administration Center
1600 Pacific Highway, #335
San Diego, CA 92101-2470
(619) 531-5533

4th District
Leon Williams—1992-1994
County Administration Center
1600 Pacific Highway, #335
San Diego, CA 92101-2470

(619) 531-5544

5th District
John MacDonald—1990-1994
County Administration Center
1600 Pacific Highway, #335
San Diego, CA 92101-2470
(619) 531-5555
District Address
325 South Melrose Drive
Vista, CA 92083-6627
(619) 940-4660

Other Elected County Officials

Assessor
Gregory J. Smith—1992-1994
County Administration Center
1600 Pacific Highway, Rm 103
San Diego, CA 92101-2480
(619) 531-5507
FAX (619) 557-4056

District Attorney
Edwin L. Miller, Jr.—1992-1994
County Courthouse
220 West Broadway, 7th Floor
(mail) 101 West Broadway, #1440
San Diego, CA 92101-8287
(619) 531-4040
FAX (619) 531-3735

Recorder/County Clerk
Annette J. Evans—1992-1994
County Administration Center
1600 Pacific Highway, Rm 260
San Diego, CA 92101-2422
(Mail) PO Box 1750
(619) 237-0502
FAX (619) 557-4155

Sheriff
Jim Roache—1992-1994
9621 Ridgehaven Court
San Diego, CA 92123-1636

COUNTY PLANNING COMMISSION 694-3816

(Mail) PO Box 429000
San Diego, CA 92124-9000
(619) 974-2222

Treasurer/Tax Collector
Paul Boland—1992-1994
County Administration Center
1600 Pacific Highway, Rm 162
San Diego, CA 92101-2479
(619) 236-3121
FAX (619) 531-6056

Chief Administrative Officer
David Janssen—*(Appointed)*
County Administration Center
1600 Pacific Highway, Rm 209
San Diego, CA 92101-2472
(619) 531-5250
FAX (619) 557-4060
(619) 231-9712
(619) 525-4641
FAX (213) 620-4467

Incorporated Cities

CARLSBAD
City of Carlsbad
1200 Carlsbad Village Drive
Carlsbad, CA 92008-1989
(619) 434-2820
FAX (619) 434-1987
(Incorporated 1952)

Mayor
Claude "Bud" Lewis—1990-1994
Council
Julie Nygaard—1990-1994
Margaret Stanton—1990-1994
Ramona Finnila—1992-1996
Ann Kulchin—1992-1996
Treasurer
Jim Stanton—1990-1994
City Clerk
Aletha Rautenkranz—1990-1994

City Manager
Ray Patchett—*(Appointed)*

Regular Election Scheduled:
November, Even Years.

CHULA VISTA
City of Chula Vista
276 Fourth Avenue
Chula Vista, CA 91910-2631
(619) 691-5031
FAX (619) 425-6184
(Incorporated 1911)

Mayor
Tim Nader—*1991-1994
Council
Jerry Rindone—-*Seat 1*, 1990-1994
Leonard Moore—-*Seat 2*, 1990-1994
Shirley Horton—*Seat 3*, 1992-1996
Robert Fox—-*Seat 4*, 1992-1996
City Clerk
Beverly Authelet—*(Appointed)*
City Manager
John D. Goss—*(Appointed)*

Regular Election Scheduled:
*Primary: June, Even Year (can win in
June with over 50% of vote. Otherwise,
run-off in November.)
General: November, Even Year.
Mayor elected by Special Election.

CORONADO
City of Coronado
1825 Strand Way
Coronado, CA 92118-3099
(619) 522-7320
FAX (619) 437-0371
(Incorporated 1890)

Mayor
Mary Herron—1992-1996
Council
Susan Keith—1990-1994

Robert Chamberlain—1990-1994
Thomas Smisek—1992-1996
Ruth K. "Patty" Schmidt—1992-1996
City Clerk
Jacqueline A. Wilson—*(Appointed)*
City Manager
Homer Bludau—*(Appointed)*

Regular Election Scheduled:
November, Even Years.

DEL MAR
City of Del Mar
1050 Camino Del Mar
Del Mar, CA 92014-2604
(619) 755-9313
FAX (619) 755-2794
(Incorporated 1959)

Mayor
Rod Franklin—*1992-1993
Council
Rod Franklin—1990-1994
Ellliot Parks—**1991-1994
Jan McMillan—1992-1996
Henry D.I. Abarbanel—1992-1996
Edward Colbert—1992-1996
City Clerk
Patti Barnes—*(Appointed)*
City Manager
Lauraine Brekke-Esparza—*(Appointed)*

Regular Election Scheduled:
April, Even Years.
* *Selected by Council from*
Councilmembers each April for one-year
term.
** *Appointed.*

EL CAJON
City of El Cajon
200 East Main Street
El Cajon, CA 92020-3912
(619) 441-1776
FAX (619) 441-1537

(Incorporated 1912)

Mayor
Joan Shoemaker—1990-1994
Council
Harriet Stockwell—1990-1994
W.E. "Bob" McClellan—1992-1996
Richard J. Ramos—1992-1996
Mark Lewis—1992-1996
City Clerk
Marilynn Linn—*(Appointed)*
City Manager
Robert Acker—*(Appointed)*

Regular Election Scheduled:
June, Even Years.

ENCINITAS
City of Encinitas
505 South Vulcan Avenue
Encinitas, CA 92024-3633
(619) 633-2600
FAX (619) 633-2627
(Incorporated 1986)

Mayor
John Davis—*1992-1993
Council
John Davis—1990-1994
Maura Wiegand—1990-1994
Gail Hano—1992-1996
Chuck Du Vivier—1992-1996
James Bond—1992-1996
City Clerk
Jane Pool—*(Appointed)*
City Manager
Warren Shafer—*(Appointed)*

Regular Election scheduled:
November, Even Years.
**Selected by Council from Concilmembers*
each November for one-year term.

ESCONDIDO
City of Escondido

201 North Broadway
Escondido, CA 92025-2709
(619) 741-4880
FAX (619) 741-7541
(Incorporated 1888)

Mayor
Jerry Harmon—* 1992-1994
Council
Sid Hollins—1990-1994
Lori Holt Pfeiler—1992-1996
Elmer C. Cameron—1992-1996
Rick Foster—1992-1996
Treasurer
Kenneth Hugins—1992-1996
City Clerk
Jeanne Bunch—1992-1996
City Manager
Douglas K. Clark—*(Appointed)*

Regular Election Scheduled:
June, Even Years.
*Two-year term.

IMPERIAL BEACH
City of Imperial Beach
825 Imperial Beach Boulevard
Imperial Beach, CA 91932-2702
(619) 423-8300
(Incorporated 1956)

Mayor
Michael B. Bixler—1990-1994
Council
Marti Goethe—1990-1994
Jay Robbins—1990-1994
Diane Rose—1992-1996
Steven Haskins—1992-1996
City Clerk
Cynthia Tjarks—*(Appointed)*
City Manager
Ronald C. Jack—*(Appointed)*

Regular Election Scheduled:
November, Even Years.

LA MESA
City of La Mesa
8130 Allison Avenue
La Mesa, CA 91941-5002
PO Box 937
La Mesa, CA 91941-0937
(619) 463-6611
FAX (619) 462-7528
(Incorporated 1912)

Mayor
Art Madrid—1990-1994
Council
Barry Jantz—1990-1994
Jay LaSuer—1990-1994
Ruth Sterling—1992-1996
Donna Alm—1992-1996
Treasurer
Kenneth W. Trent—1990-1994
City Clerk
Anita Underwood—1992-1996
City Manager
David Wear—*(Appointed)*

Regular Election Scheduled:
November, Even Years.

LEMON GROVE
City of Lemon Grove
3232 Main Street
Lemon Grove, CA 91945-1705
(619) 464-6934
FAX (619) 460-3716
(Incorporated 1977)

Mayor
Brian Cochran—* 1992-1994
Council
Brian Cochran—1990-1994
Craig Lake —1990-1994
Lois Heiserman—1990-1994
Robert F. "Bob" Burns—1992-1996
Jerome Legerton—1992-1996
Finance Director/City Clerk
Christine Taub—*(Appointed)*

City Manager
Jack Shelver—*(Appointed)*

Regular Election Scheduled:
June, Even Years.
*Selected by Council from
Councilmembers in July, even years for
two-year term.

NATIONAL CITY
City of National City
1243 National City Boulevard
National City, CA 91950-4397
(619) 336-4200
FAX (619) 336-4376
(Incorporated 1887)

Mayor
George Waters—1990-1994
Council
Michael Dalla—1990-1994
Rosalie Zarate—1990-1994
Ralph Inzunza—1992-1996
Ron Morrison—1992-1996
Treasurer
George Hood—1992-1996
City Clerk
Lori Anne Peoples—1992-1996
City Manager
Tom G. McCabe—*(Appointed)*

Regular Election Scheduled
November, Even Years.

OCEANSIDE
City of Oceanside
300 North Hill Street
Oceanside, CA 92054-2824
(619) 966-4460
FAX (619) 966-4436
(Incorporated 1888)

Mayor
Dick Lyon—1992-1996

Council
Colleen R. O'Harra—1992-1996
Terry W. Johnson—1992-1996
Nancy York—1992-1994
Don Rodee—1990-1994
Treasurer
Rosemary R. Jones—1992-1996
City Clerk
Barbara Riegel Wayne—1992-1996
City Manager
Jim Turner (Interim)—*(Appointed)*

Regular Election Scheduled:
November, Even Years.

POWAY
City of Poway
13325 Civic Center Drive
Poway, CA 92064-5755
PO Box 789
Poway, CA 92074-0789
(619) 748-6600 or
(619) 695-1400
FAX (619) 748-1455
(Incorporated 1980)

Mayor
Don Higginson—*1992-1994
Council
Tony Snesko—1990-1994
Bob Emery—1992-1996
Susan Callery—1992-1996
Mickey Cafagna—**1992-1994
City Clerk/Treasurer
Marjorie Wahlsten—*(Appointed)*
City Manager
James Bowersox—*(Appointed)*

Regular Election Sscheduled:
November, Even Years.
*Two-year term.
**Appointed.

SAN DIEGO
City of San Diego

202 C Street
San Diego, CA 92101-4806
City Clerk (619) 533-4000
Council (619) 236-6440
FAX (619) 533-4045
(Incorporated 1850)

Mayor
Susan Golding—1992-1996
Council-District 1
Abbe Wolfsheimer—1989-1993
Council-District 2
Ron Roberts—1991-1995
Council-District 3
John Hartley—1989-1993
Council-District 4
George Stevens—1991-1995
Council-District 5
Tom Behr—* 1991-1993
Council-District 6
Valerie Stallings—1991-1995
Council-District 7
Judy McCarty—1989-1993
Council-District 8
Juan Vargas—* 1993-1993
City Attorney
John Witt—1992-1996
City Clerk
Charles Abdelnour—(Appointed)
City Manager
Jack McGrory—*(Appointed)*

Regular Election Scheduled:
Council:
Primary-September, Odd Year.
General-November, Odd Year.
(Council elected or nominated by district
in September; can win with over 50% of
the vote.
Otherwise, run-off by district in
November.)
Mayor/City Attorney:
Primary-June, Even Year.
General-November, Even Year.
(Election held at same time as Presiden-

tial election. Can win in June with over
50% of the vote.
Otherwise, run-off in November.)
*Elected by Special Elections.

SAN MARCOS
City of San Marcos
105 West Richmar Avenue
San Marcos, CA 92069-1699
(619) 744-1050
FAX (619) 744-7543
(Incorporated 1963)

Mayor
Lee Thibadeau—1990-1994
Council
Mark Loscher—1990-1994
Pia Harris—1990-1994
F.H. "Corky" Smith—1992-1996
Betty Evans—1992-1996
City Clerk
Sheila A. Kennedy—*(Appointed)*
City Manager/Treasurer
Richard W. Gittings—*(Appointed)*

Regular Election Scheduled:
November, Even years.

SANTEE
City of Santee
10765 Woodside Avenue
Santee, CA 92071-3198
(619) 258-4100
(Incorporated 1980)

Mayor
Jack E. Dale—1992-1996
Council
James A. Romine—1992-1996
Jim Bartell—1990-1994
Hal Ryan—1990-1994
Edith A. French—*1993-1994
City Clerk
Loretta H. Roper—*(Appointed)*

City Manager
Ronald L. Ballard—*(Appointed)*

Regular Election Scheduled:
November, Even Years.
*Appointed

SOLANA BEACH
City of Solana Beach
380 Stevens Avenue, #305
Solana Beach, CA 92075-2068
(619) 755-2998
FAX (619) 792-6513
(Incorporated 1986)

Mayor
Margaret Schlesinger—* 1992-1993
Council
Margaret Schlesinger —1990-1994
Paul Tompkins—1990-1994
Teri Renteria—1992-1996
Marion B. Dodson—1992-1996
Joe Kellejian—1992-1996
City Clerk
Deborah Harrington—*(Appointed)*
City Manager
Michael W. Huse—*(Appointed)*

Regular Election Scheduled:
November, Even Year.
*Selected by Council from
Councilmembers each December for
one-year term.

VISTA
City of Vista
600 Eucalyptus
Vista, CA 92084-6240
(619) 726-1340
FAX (619) 945-7859
(Incorporated 1963)

Mayor
Gloria E. McClellan—1990-1994
Council
Dal Williams—1990-1994

Jeanette M. Smith—1990-1994
Ted Cole—1992-1996
Scott Papckard—1992-1996
City Clerk
Jo Seibert
City Manager
Morris B. Vance

Regular Election Scheduled:
November, Even Years.

PARK & RECREATION DEPARTMENTS

Carlsbad—434-2824
1200 Carlsbad Village Dr.
Carlsbad, CA 92008

Chula Vista—691-5071
276 Fourth Ave.
Chula Vista, CA 91910

Coronado—522-7342
1845 Strand Way
Coronado, CA 92118

Del Mar—755-9313
1050 Camino Del Mar
Del Mar, CA 92014

El Cajon—441-1744
200 E. Main St.
El Cajon, CA 92020

Encinitas—633-2740
505 S. Vulcan Ave.
Encinitas, CA 92024

Escondido—741-4691
201 N. Broadway
Escondido, CA 92025

Imperial Beach—423-8300
825 Imperial Beach Blvd.
Imperial Beach, CA 91932

La Mesa—469-4128
4975 Memorial Dr.
La Mesa, CA 91941

Lemon Grove—668-4575
3146 School Lane
Lemon Grove, CA 91945

National City—336-4290
140 E. 12th St. Suite A
National City, CA 91950

Oceanside—966-4530
300 N. Hill St.
Oceanside, CA 92054

Poway—679-4342
P.O. Box 789
Poway, CA 92074

San Diego—236-6643
City Administration Building
202 C Street, MS 9B
San Diego, CA 92101

San Marcos—737-9363
105 W. Richmar
San Marcos, CA 92069

Santee—258-4180
10144 Mission Gorge Rd.
Santee CA 92071

Solana Beach—793-2998
380 Stevens Ave. #305
Solana Beach, CA 92075

Vista—726-1340
P.O. Box 1988
Vista, CA 92085

County of San Diego—694-3049
5201 Ruffin Rd. Suite P
San Diego, CA 92123

STATE OF CALIFORNIA
Department of Parks and Recreation
3990 Old Town Ave., Suite 300
San Diego, CA 92110
220-5422

San Diego Jack Murphy Stadium
Stadium Authority
Tawfiq N. Khoury, Chair
9449 Friars Rd.
San Diego, CA 92108
525-8282/ FAX 283-0460

San Diego Convention Center
Carol Wallace, General Manager
111 W. Harbor Drive
San Diego, CA 92101
525-5000/ FAX 525-5005

San Diego Metropolitan Transit
Development Board (SDMTD)
James Mills, Board Chairman
1255 Imperial Ave., Ste. 1000
San Diego, CA 92101
231-1466/ FAX 234-3407
Customer complaints 233-3004

San Diego Unified Port District
P.O. Box 488
San Diego, CA 92112
686-6200/ FAX 291-0753

DEAD ANIMAL REMOVAL

Carlsbad—438-2722 x134
M-Th 7:30 am-5:30 pm,
F 8 am - 5 pm
No pick up from private property,
442-3287
Chula Vista—691-5123
M-F 9am-5pm, Sat 9am-12noon
No pick up from private property,
call 442-3287

Caltrans *(State Hwys, 805, 94, 5, 8)*

688-6785
M-F 8am-5pm
After hours emergencies (CHP)
237-6812

Coronado—522-7371
Sun-Sat 8am-4pm
After hours 4pm-8pm call police 522-7350
Will pick up from private property
during working hours

Del Mar—755-3294
M-F 7:30am-4pm
No pick up from private property,
call 442-3287

El Cajon—448-7383
T-Sat 10am-6pm
Will pick up from private property

Encinitas, Cardiff, Leucadia
(Tri-Cities)—442-3287
Private contractor will pick up 24 hrs/day
Will pick up from private property for a
fee

Escondido—745-4362
M-Sat 8am-4pm
Will pick up from private property for
$20 fee

Imperial Beach—691-5123
Under contract with Chula Vista (same
hrs.)
No pick up from private property,
call 442-3287

La Mesa—469-6111 x 243
Will pick up from private property

Lemon Grove—464-6934
M-F 8am-5pm
No pick up from private property,
call 442-3287

National City—336-4411
M-F 8am-5pm
Will pick up from private property Sun-T

Oceanside—757-4357
M-F 8am-5pm
Will pick up from private property
strays - no fee; pets - $15

Poway—279-8242
Private contractor will pick up 24 hrs/day
Will pick up from private property for a
fee
D&D 279-8242 or D.A.R. 442-3287

San Diego—492-5055
M-F 8am-5pm
No pick up from private property,
call 442-3287

San Marcos—752-7550 x3331
M-F 7am-3:30pm
No pick up from private property,
call 442-3287

Santee—442-3287
Private contractor will pick up 24 hrs/day
Will pick up from private property for a
fee

Solana Beach—390-0333
Private contractor will pick up 24 hrs/day
Will pick up from private property for a
fee
A.A. 390-0333 or D.A.R. 442-3287

Vista—757-4357
Under contract with Oceanside
Will pick up from private property *(see
Oceanside)*

Unincorporated County—442-3287
Private contractor will pick up 24 hrs/day
Will pick up from private property for a
fee

CHAMBERS OF COMMERCE

Chula Vista—420-6602
233 Fourth Ave.
Chula Vista, CA 91910

Coronado—435-9260
P.O. Box 180396
Coronado, CA 92178-0396

Del Mar—755-4844
1442 Camino del Mar, Ste. 214
Del Mar, CA 92014

El Cajon—440-6161
109 Rea Ave.
El Cajon, CA 92020

Escondido—745-2125
P.O. Box C
Escondidio, CA 92033

Greater San Diego
La Jolla—450-1518
4275 Executive Square Ste. 920
La Jolla, CA 92037
San Diego—232-0124
402 W. Broadway, Ste. 1000
San Diego, CA 92101

La Mesa—465-7700
8155 University Ave.
La Mesa, CA 91941

School Districts

County Board of Education
6401 Linda Vista Road
San Diego, CA 92111-7399
(619) 292-3515/FAX (619) 268-5864

District 1
Barbara Carpenter—1992-1996
District 2

Joe Rindone—1992-1996
District 3
Martin Block—1990-1994
District 4
Jim Kelly—1992-1996
District 5
Bill R. Hampton—1990-1994
Superintendent
Harry C. Weinberg—*(Appointed)*

Regular Elections Schduled:
Districts 1, 2 and 4 June/November Even Years with Presidential election.
Districts 3 and 5 June/November Even Years with Gubernatorial election.

San Diego Community College District
3375 Camino Del Rio South
San Diego, CA 92108-3883
(619) 584-6500/FAX (619) 584-7313

District A
Maria Senour—1990-1994
District B
Fred Colby—1992-1996
District C
Kara Kobey—1990-1994
District D
Evonne Schulze—1992-1996
District E
Denise Moreno Ducheny—1990-1994
Chancellor
Augustine Gallego—*(Appointed)*

Regular Election Scheduled:
Districts B and D June/November Even Years with Presidential election.
Districts A, C and E June/November Even Years with Gubernatorial election.

San Diego Unified School District
4100 Normal Street
San Diego, CA 92103-2682
(619) 293-8686/FAX (619) 293-8267

District A
Ann Armstong—1992-1996
District B
Sue Bruan—1990-1994
District C
John de Beck—1990-1994
District D
Ron Ottinger—1992-1996
District E
Shirley Weber—1992-1996
Superintendent
Dr. Thomas W. Payzant—*(Appointed)*

Regular Elections Scheduled:
Districts A, D and E with June/November
Even Years with Presidential election.

Alpine Union
1323 Administration Way
Alpine, CA 91901-9401
(619) 445-3236/FAX (619) 445-7045

Bonsall Union
31505 Old River Road
PO Box 3
Bonsall, CA 92003-0003
(619) 631-5200/FAX (619) 941-4409

Borrego Springs Unified
2281 Diegueno Road
PO Box 235
Borrego Springs, CA 92004-0235
(619) 767-5357/FAX (619) 767-5999

Cajon Valley Union
189 Roanoke Road
PO Box 1007
El Cajon, CA 92022-1007
(619) 588-3000/FAX (619) 588-7653

Cardiff
1888 Montgomery Avenue
Cardiff, CA 92007-2399
(619) 632-5890/FAX (619) 942-5831

Carlsbad Unified
801 Pine Avenue
Carlsbad, CA 92008-2493
(619) 729-9291/FAX (619) 729-9685

Chula Vista Elementary
84 East J Street
Chula Vista, CA 91910-6199
(619) 425-9600/FAX (619) 427-0463

Coronado Unified
555 D Avenue
Coronado, CA 92118-1714
(619) 522-8900

Dehesa
4612 Dehesa Road
El Cajon, CA 92019-2922
(619) 444-2161/FAX (619) 444-2105

Del Mar Union
225 Ninth Street
Del Mar, CA 92014-2716
(619) 755-9301/FAX (619) 755-4361

Encinitas Union
101 South Rancho Santa Fe Road
Encinitas, CA 92024-4308
(619) 944-4300/FAX (619) 942-7094

Escondido Union
1330 East Grand Avenue
Escondido, CA 92027-3099
(619) 745-7000/FAX (619) 745-8896

Escondido Union High
240 South Maple Street
Escondido, CA 92025-4182
(619) 480-3000/FAX (619) 480-3184

Fallbrook Union Elementary
321 North Iowa Street
PO Box 698
Fallbrook, CA 92088-0698
(619) 723-7000/FAX (619) 723-2507

Fallbrook Union High
2400 Stage Coach Lane
PO Box 368
Fallbrook, CA 92088-0368
(619) 723-6300/FAX (619) 723-6343

Grossmont-Cuyamaca
Community College
8800 Grossmont College Drive
El Cajon, CA 92020-1799
(619) 465-1700/FAX (619) 461-3396

Grossmont Union High
1100 Murray Drive
PO Box 1043
La Mesa, CA 91944-1043
(619) 465-3131

Jamul-Dulzura Union
14581 Lyons Valley Road
Jamul, CA 91935-9701
(619) 669-1400/FAX (619) 669-0254

Julian Union
1704 Highway 78
PO Box 337
Julian, CA 92036-0337
(619) 765-0661/FAX (619) 765-0220

Julian Union High
1656 Highway 78
PO Box 417
Julian, CA 92036-0417
(619) 765-0606/FAX (619) 765-2926

La Mesa-Spring Valley
4750 Date Avenue
La Mesa, CA 91941-5214
(619) 668-5700

Lakeside Union
12335 Woodside Avenue
PO Box 578
Lakeside, CA 92040-0578
(619) 390-2600

Lemon Grove
8025 Lincoln Street
Lemon Grove, CA 91945-2515
(619) 589-5600/FAX (619) 462-7959

MiraCosta Community Collge
One Barnard Drive
Oceanside, CA 92056-3820
(619) 757-2121/FAX (619) 575-2601

Mountain Empire Unified
3291 Buckman Springs Road
Pine Valley, CA 91962-4003
(619) 445-8234

National
1500 N Avenue
National City, CA 91950-0150
(619) 474-6791/FAX (619) 477-5144

Oceanside Unified
2111 Mission Avenue
Oceanside, CA 92054-2326
(619) 757-2560

Palomar Community College
1140 West Mission Road
San Marcos, CA 92069-1487
(619) 744-1150

Pauma
33158 Cole Grade Road
PO Box 409
Pauma Valley, CA 92061-0409
(619) 742-3741/FAX (619) 742-1214

Poway Unified
13626 Twin Peaks Road
Poway, CA 92064-3034
(619) 586-7500 or
(619) 748-0010

Ramona Unified
720 9th Street
Ramona, CA 92065-2348

151

(619) 788-5000
FAX (619) 789-9168

Rancho Santa Fe
5927 La Granada at El Fuego
PO Box 809
Rancho Santa Fe, CA 92067-0809
(619) 756-1141/FAX (619) 759-0912

San Diego Community College
3375 Camino del Rio South
San Diego, CA 92108-3883
(619) 584-6500/FAX (619) 584-7513
Regular Election Scheduled:
November, Even Years.

San Diego Unified
4100 Normal Street
San Diego, CA 92103-2683
(619) 293-8686/FAX (619) 293-8267

San Dieguito Union High
710 Encinitas Boulevard
Encinitas, CA 92024-3357
(619) 753-6491

San Marcos Unified
270 San Marcos Boulevard
San Marcos, CA 92069-1290
(619) 744-4776/FAX (619) 471-4928

San Pasqual Union
16666 San Pasqual Valley Road
Escondido, CA 92027-7001
(619) 745-4931/FAX (619) 745-2473

San Ysidro
4350 Otay Mesa Road
San Ysidro, CA 92173-1685
(619) 428-4476/FAX (619) 428-9355

Santee
9625 Cuyamaca Street
PO Box 719007
Santee, CA 92072-9007
(619) 258-2300

Solana Beach
309 North Rios Avenue
Solana Beach, CA 92075-1298
(619) 755-8000/FAX (619) 755-0814

South Bay Union
601 Elm Avenue
Imperial Beach, CA 91932-2098
(619) 575-5900

Southwestern Community College
900 Otay Lakes Road
Chula Vista, CA 91910-7297
(619) 421-6700/FAX (619) 482-6323

Spencer Valley
4414 Highway 78 & 79
PO Box 159
Santa Ysabel, CA 92070-0159
(619) 765-0336

Sweetwater Union High
1130 Fifth Avenue
Chula Vista, CA 91911-2098
(619) 691-5500/FAX (619) 420-0339

Vallecitos
5211 Fifth Street
Fallbrook, CA 92028-9796
(619) 728-7092

Valley Center Union
28751 Cole Grade Road
Valley Center, CA 92082-6599
(619) 749-0464/FAX (619) 749-1208

Vista Unified
1234 Arcadia Avenue
Vista, CA 92084-3404
(619) 726-2170

Warner Union
Highway 79
PO Box 8
Warner Springs, CA 92086-0008
(619) 782-3517

Regular Election Scheduled:
November, Even Years.

Special Districts

Alpine Community Planning
PO Box 819
Alpine, CA 91903-1600
(619) 445-4526

Alpine Fire Protection
1834 Alpine Boulevard
Alpine, CA 91901-2107
(619) 445-2636/FAX (619) 445-2634

Bonita-Sunnyside Fire Protection
4900 Bonita Road
Bonita, CA 91902-1725
(619) 479-2346/FAX (619) 479-2393

Borrego Springs Fire Protection
2324 Stirrup Road
PO Box 898
Borrego Springs, CA 92004-0898
(619) 767-5436/FAX (619) 767-5193

**Borrego Springs Park
Community Services**
3064 Borrego Valley Road
PO Box 306
Borrego Springs, CA 92004-0306
(619) 767-3693

Borrego Water
PO Box 369
Vista, CA 92085-0369
(619) 726-5856

Bostonia Fire Protection
1273 Clarendon Street
El Cajon, CA 92021-4919
(619) 588-8112/FAX (619) 442-3789

Bueno Colorado Municipal Water
202 West Connecticut Avenue

Vista, CA 92083-3645
(619) 726-1535/FAX (619) 724-0856

Canebrake County Water
140 Smoketree Lane
Julian, CA 92036-9336
(619) 765-1810

Crest Fire Protection
1811 Suncrest Boulevard
El Cajon, CA 92021-4246
(619) 579-6034/FAX (619) 579-1148

**Crest/Dehesa/Harbison Canyon/
Granite Hills Community Planning**
1110 Old Mountain View Road
El Cajon, CA 92021-7838
(619) 447-3138

Cuyamaca Water *(Landowner)*
PO Box 609
Julian, CA 92036-0609
(619) 765-1202/FAX (619) 765-3300

Deer Springs Fire Protection
8709 Circle R Drive
Escondido, CA 92026-5802
(619) 749-8001/FAX (619) 749-8003

Descanso Community Water
25077 Viejas Boulevard
PO Box 610
Descanso, CA 91916-0610
(619) 445-2330

Fairbanks Ranch Community Services
605 Third Street
Encinitas, CA 92024-3513
(619) 942-5147/FAX (619) 632-0164

Fallbrook Community Planning
205 Calle Linda
Fallbrook, CA 92028-9425
(619) 728-8081

Fallbrook Hospital
624 East Elder
Fallbrook, CA 92028-3099
(619) 728-1191

Fallbrook Public Utility
PO Box 2290
Fallbrook, CA 92088-2290
(619) 728-1125

Fallbrook Sanitary
431 South Main Street
Fallbrook, CA 92028-2993
(619) 728-8319/FAX (619) 728-5821

***Greater Mountain Empire
Resource Conservation**
1132 North Second Street
El Cajon, CA 92021-5008
(619) 442-0559/FAX (619) 442-2917

Grossmont Hospital
5555 Grossmont Center Drive
La Mesa, CA 91942-3019
PO Box 158
La Mesa, CA 91944-0158
(619) 465-0711/FAX (619) 461-7191

Helix Water (Irrigation)
8111 University Avenue
PO Box 518
La Mesa, CA 91944-0518
(619) 466-0585

Jacumba Community Services
1266 Railroad Avenue
PO Box 425
Jacumba, CA 91934-0425
(619) 766-4359

Jamul-Dulzura Community Planning
PO Box 613
Jamul, CA 91935-0613
(619) 463-6393

Julian Community Planning
PO Box 249
Julian, CA 929036-0249
(619) 765-2726

Julian Community Services
2656 Farmer Road
PO Box 681
Julian, CA 92036-0681
(619) 765-0483/FAX (619) 765-1680

Julian-Cuyamaca Fire Protection
2645 Farmer Road
PO Box 33
Julian, CA 92036-0033
(619) 765-1510/FAX (619) 765-1680

Lakeside Community Planning
PO Box 2040
Lakeside, CA 92040-2040
(619) 561-6323

Lakeside Fire Protection
12365 Parkside Stree
Lakeside, CA 92040-3006
(619) 390-2350/FAX (619) 443-1568
Regular Election Scheduled:
November, Even Years.
**No election, candidates file for office
and appointments are made by the Board
of Supervisors.*

Lakeside Water *(Irrigation)*
9739 Los Coches road
PO Box 638
Lakeside, CA 92040-0638
(619) 443-3805/FAX (619) 443-3690

Leucadia County Water
1960 La Costa Avenue
Carlsbad, CA 92009-6810
PO Box 2397
Leucadia, CA 92023-2397
(619) 753-0155

Lower Sweetwater Fire Protection
2711 Granger Avenue
National City, CA 91950-7824
(619) 470-4557

*Mission Resource Conservation
1181 East Mission Road
Fallbrook, CA 92028-2230
(619) 728-1332/FAX (619) 723-5316

Mootamai Municipal Water
34928 Valley Center Road
PO Box 177
Pauma Valley, CA 92061-0177
(619) 742-3704/FAX (619) 742-2069

Morro Hills Community Services
PO Box 161
Fallbrook, CA 92088-0161
(619) 723-3642

North County Fire Protection
315 East Ivy Street
Fallbrook, CA 92028-2138
(619) 723-2005/FAX (619) 723-2004

Olivenhain Municipal Water
1966 Olivehain Road
Encinitas, CA 92024-5676
(619) 753-6466/FAX (619) 753-1578

Otay Water *(Municipal)*
10595 Jamacha Boulevard
Spring Valley, CA 91977-7202
(619) 670-2222/FAX (619) 670-2258

Padre Dam Municipal Water
10887 Woodside Avenue
PO Box 719003
Santee, CA 92072-9003
(619) 448-3111/FAX (619) 449-9469

Palomar Pomerado Health System
215 South Hickory Street, #310
Escondido, CA 92025-4359

(619) 739-2100/FAX (619) 739-2115

*Palomar-Ramona-Julian Resource Conservation
332 South Juniper Street, #110
Escondido, CA 92025-4941
(619) 745-2061/FAX (619) 745-3210

Pauma Municipal Water
15658 Hioghway 76
Pauma Valley, CA 92061-4548
(619) 742-3316

Pauma Valley Community Services
16160 Highway 76
PO Box 434
Pauma Valley, CA 92061-0434
(619) 742-1909/FAX (619) 742-1588

Pine Valley Fire Protection
28850 Old Highway 80
PO Box 130
Pine Valley, CA 91962-0130
(619) 473-8445/FAX (619) 473-3243

Questhaven Municipal Water
20560 Questhaven Road
Escondido, CA 92029-4810
(619) 744-1500/FAX (619) 744-1500

Rainbow Community Planning
6441 Rainbow Heights Road
Fallbrook CA 92028-9620
(619) 728-8730/FAX (619) 723-2030

Rainbow Municipal Water
3707 South Highway 395
PO Box 2500
Fallbrook, CA 92088-2500
(619) 728-1178/FAX (619) 728-2527

Ramona Community Planning
215 6th Street
Ramona, CA 92065-2011
(619) 788-2123/FAX (619) 741-0396

155

Ramona Municipal Water
105 Earlham Street
Ramona, CA 92065-1599
(619) 789-1330/FAX (619) 788-2202

Rancho Santa Fe Community Services
605 Third Street
Encinitas, CA 92024-3513
(619) 942-5147

Rancho Santa Fe Fire Protection
16936 El Fuego/PO Box 410
Rancho Santa Fe, CA 92067-0410
(619) 756-5971/FAX (619) 756-4799

Rincon Del diablo Municipal Water
1920 North Iris Lane
Escondido, CA 92026-1318
(619) 745-5522/FAX (619) 745-4235

Rincon Ranch Community Services
34928 Valley Center Road
PO Box 882
Pauma Valley, CA 92061-0882
(619) 742-1330/FAX (619) 742-2069

Riverview Water *(Landowner)*
11769 Waterhill Road
Lakeside, CA 92040-2998
(619) 561-1333/FAX (619) 561-1659

Rural Fire Protection
13910 Lyons Valley Road, #R
Jamul, CA 91935-2028
(619) 669-1188/FAX (619) 669-1798

San Dieguito Community Planning
PO Box 2789
Rancho Santa Fe, CA 92067-2789
(619) 489-0900

San Luis Rey Municipal Water
5328 Highway 76
Bonsall, CA 92003-2306
(619) 728-1434

**San Miguel Consolidated
Fire Protection**
2850 Via Orange Way
Spring Valley, CA 91978-1746
(619) 670-0500/FAX (619) 670-5331

Santa Fe Irrigation
5920 Linea Del Cielo
PO Box 409
Rancho Santa Fe, CA 92067-0409
(619) 756-2424/FAX (619) 756-0450

South Bay Irrigation
505 Garrett Avenue
PO Box 2328
Chula Vista, CA 92912-2328
(619) 427-0868/FAX (619) 425-7469

Spring Valley Community Planning
PO Box 1637
Spring Valley, CA 91979-1637
(619) 475-6432

Sweetwater Community Planning
PO Box 460
Bonita, CA 91908-0460
(619) 479-0665

Tijuana Valley County Water
2222 Coronado Avenue, #F
San Diego, CA 92154-2037
(619) 429-6106/FAX (619) 429-4186

Tri-City Hospital
4002 Vista Way
Oceanside, CA 92056-4506
(619) 940-3348/FAX (619) 724-1010

***Upper San Luis Rey
Resource Conservation**
1181 East Mission Road
Fallbrook, CA 92028-2231
(619) 728-1332/FAX (619) 723-5316

Valle De Oro Community Planning
PO Box 3958
La Mesa, CA 91944-3958
(619) 670-0986

Vallecitos Water
788 San Marcos Boulevard
San Marcos, CA 92069-4222
(619) 744-0460/FAX (619) 744-3507

Valley Center Community Planning
PO Box 127
Valley Center, CA 92082-0127
(619) 749-4586/FAX (619) 749-5442

Valley Center Community Services
28246 Lilac Road
PO Box 141
Valley Center, CA 92082-0141
(619) 749-8852/FAX (619) 749-6075

Valley Center Fire Protection
28234 Lilac Road
Valley Center, CA 92082-5413
(619) 751-7600/FAX (619) 749-3892

Valley Center Municipal Water
29300 Valley Center Road
PO Box 67
Valley Center, CA 92082-0067
(619) 749-1600/FAX (619) 749-6478

Vista Fire Protection
122-201 Escondido Avenue
Vista, CA 92084-6040
(619) 758-3815/FAX (619) 758-2628

Vista Irrigation
202 West Connecticut Avenue
Vista, CA 92083-3645
(619) 724-8811

Whispering Palms
Community Services
605 Third Street

Encinitas, CA 92024-3513
(619) 942-5147/FAX (619) 632-0164

Wynola Water (Landowner)
PO Box 193
Santa Ysabel, CA 92070-0193
(619) 765-0109

Yuima Municipal Water
34928 Valley Center Road
PO Box 177
Pauma Valley, CA 92061-0177
(619) 742-3705/FAX (619) 742 -2069

Political Parties

American Independent
8158 Palm Street
Lemon Grove, CA 91945-3028
(619) 460-4484

Democratic
957 23rd Street
San Diego, CA 92102-1913
(619) 238-1174

Green
PO Box 128684
San Diego, CA 92112-8684
(619) 233-4442

Libertarian
PO Box 16449
San Diego, CA 92176-6449
(619) 276-1776/FAX (619) 274-1776

Peace & Freedom
PO Box 19735
San Diego, CA 92159-9735
(619) 685-7331

Republican
1399 9th Avenue, #211
San Diego, CA 92101-4733
(619) 236-1990

Agencies

U.S. GOVERNMENT AGENCIES

Federal Information Center
(800) 726-4995
American Consulate General *(Tijuana)*
-011-52-66-81-7400
Army Reserve Center
283-5571
Border Patrol
San Ysidro (Headquarters)—428-7251
San Clemente Checkpoint—430-7029
San Ysidro Port of Entry—428-7207
Temecula Checkpoint—(714) 676-2261
Coast Guard Public Affairs
557-6556
Coast Guard Search & Rescue
295-3121
Customs Agency
San Ysidro—428-7201
Tecate—478-5356
Defense Department
557-5544
FBI
231-1122
FCC
268-0977
Federal District Court Clerk
557-5600
Federal Drug Enforcement Admin.
585-4200
Federal Job Information Center
557-6165
Food & Drug Administration
550-3850
Forest Service
673-6180
Housing and Urban Development
557-5305
Immigration & Naturalization Service
557-5570
Internal Revenue Service
(714)643-4069

Navy Ship Information
556-3123
Navy Shore Patrol
556-1860
Postal Service
574-0477
Secret Service
557-5640
Social Security
(800)772-1213
State Dept. Boundary and Water Comm.
428-7221
Treasury Dept./Customs
557-5360
U.S. Marshal
557-6620
U.S. Probation Office
557-6650
U.S. Veterans Assistance Center
297-8220
Weather Bureau Information
297-2107
Weather Bureau Tape
289-1212

URBAN AGENCIES

American Civil Liberties Union
297-8220
Barrio Station, Inc.
238-0314
Chicano Federation
236-1228
Community Action Partnership
(County) 338-2799
Gay Center for Social Services
692-4297
MAAC Project
474-2232
from San Diego
263-9700
Mexican & American Foundation
232-1010

NAACP
236-9078
Neighborhood House Assoc.
263-7761
Union of Pan Asian Communities
232-6454
Urban League of San Diego
263-3115

CALIFORNIA STATE AGENCIES

State of California Information Center
(213) 620-3030
State Office Information
(213)897-9900
Banking Department (complaints)
(800) 622-0620
Business -
Small Business Advocates Helpline
(916) 654-4357
Coastal Commission
521-8036
Consumers Affairs
(800) 344-9940
Controller's Office
Inheritance & Gift Tax
(916) 445-6321
Board of Equalization
1350 Front Street, San Diego
Permit Applications & Changes
525-4526
Sales and Use Tax Information
525-4485
Judicial Performance Commission
(415) 904-3650
Public Utilities Commission -
complaints (800) 649-7570
Small and Minority Business Office
(916)322-5060
Social Services Dept.
quality control—467-2350
Transportation - Caltrans
688-6699
Water Quality Control Board
265-5114

Consumer Complaints

California Office of Consumer Affairs
(800)344-9940

KFMB-TV Channel 8
P.O. Box 85888
San Diego, CA 92186
Consumer Reporter: Bob Hansen
Consumer Hotline: 495-7513
Publishes a booklet "Got a Gripe?"
available free at Price Club
and at KFMB

KGTV Channel 10
10 Troubleshooter
Box 10
San Diego, CA 92112
Include phone number — does not
accept calls

San Diego County Tobacco Smoke/
Smoking Ordinance
Complaints and Inquiries:
Write, phone or FAX complaints about
co-workers or restaurants or other
violations of the non-smoking ordinance
or sales to minors.

Department of Health
P.O. Box 85222
San Diego, CA 92186
Attn: Division of Public Health Education
236-2705/FAX 239-5920

San Diego County Citizens
Assistance and Information
202 C Street
San Diego, CA 92103
236-6047

Better Business Bureau
525 B Street, San Diego 92103
234-0966

159

Victim's Rights Center
235-4459

Automotive Repair
(800) 952-5210

NOISE ABATEMENT
*Noise complaints should be addressed to
the following offices:*

**San Diego County -
Environmental Health & Noise
Control**
P.O. Box 85261
1255 Imperial Ave.
San Diego, CA 92186
338-2095/FAX 338-2174

*Cities contracting with the County for
noise abatement services:
Encinitas, Leucadia, Cardiff, Olivenhein,
Del Mar, Solana Beach, Oceanside.*
Encinitas City Code Enforcement
633-2685

Carlsbad
Code Enforcement Officer 438-1161
Dog Barking 438-2312

Chula Vista
Barking Dog Complaints 8am-5pm
691-5123
(after 5 p.m. call police 931-2197
Zoning Enforcement and Noise
691-5280

Coronado
Call police 522-7350

El Cajon
Call police 579-3391 or
City Manager 441-1716 or
Animal Control 448-7383

Escondido
Call police 741-4722
Humane Society 745-4362
Building Code Enforcement 741-4647

Imperial Beach
Call Sheriff 585-7232
Code Enforcement 423-8223

La Mesa
Call police 469-6111

Lemon Grove
Call Sheriff 441-4100
Code Enforcement Officer 441-4100
Planning Dept. 3232 Main St., Lemon
Grove, CA 92045

National City
Call police 336-4411
Code Conformance 336-4310

Oceanside
Call police 966-4901
Dogs - Humane Society 757-4337

Poway
Code Enforcement 748-6600

San Diego
Neighborhood Compliance Code
1222 First Ave., M.S. 403
San Diego, CA 92101
236-5500/FAX 236-5920 (*requires
signature*)

San Marcos
Call Sheriff 736-2140
Dog Barking - Animal Control 438-2312

Santee
Call Sheriff 565-5200
Dogs - Community Development
562-6153
Code Enforcement Officer extention 23

Vista
Dog Barking - Humane Society
757-4357
Code Enforcement 726-1240 x3407

GRAFITTI ERADICATION
(by city)

Chula Vista
Call the Public Works Dept. (691-5027),
if public property, if private property, call
police.

Coronado
Call the Public Works Dept. (522-7380),
if public property, if private property, call
police.

Del Mar
Call the Public Works Dept. (755-3294),
if public property, if private property, call
police.

El Cajon
Call the Public Works Dept. (441-1653),
if public property, if private property, call
the buildling department for the city to
remove free through Echo program.

Imperial Beach
Call the Public Works Dept. (423-8311),
if public property, if private property, call
the hotline 575-3745 for free removal.

La Mesa
Call the Public Works Dept. (466-0405),
if public, if private, call 463-6611 x 189
to receive free paint and supplies from
the "Ban the Can" program.

Lemon Grove
Call the Public Works Dept. (464-6934),
if public property, if private property, it
will receive a lower priority.

National City
Call grafitti hotline - 336-1449

Poway
Call the Public Works Dept. (679-4040),
if public property, if private property, call
police.

Santee
Call Public Works Dept. (258-4130)

Solana Beach
Call Public Works Dept. (755-2998), if
public, if privatye, call 755-2998 and talk
to Tom Ritteer for free paint and
supplies.

San Diego
Call Hotline if public or private -
627-3333

Hotlines

STATE OF CALIFORNIA
Office of Auditor General
Fraud Hotline
(800)952-5665
Hazardous Waste Hotline
(800)698-6942

COUNTY OF SAN DIEGO
Adult Abuse Reporting
476-6266 or (800) 523-6444
Child Abuse Reporting
560-2191 (24 hrs.)
Child Protective Services 694-5191
Crisis Intervention Hotline
(mental health) 236-3339
Fraud Reporting 557-0402
Social Services General Information
696-9442
Rape and Battered Women's Hotline
233-3088
2467 E Street, San Diego 92103

CITY OF SAN DIEGO
General Information
236-5555
Citizens' Suggestion Hotline
570-1000
Grafitti Hotline
627-3333
Conservative Hotline
Voice mail for conservative groups:
meetings, products, special events.
P.O. Box 7972
Chula Vista, CA 91912
482-4830/FAX 421-7180

Law Enforcement

United States Border Patrol
3752 Beyer Blvd.
San Diego, CA 92143
428-7251

Law Enforcement Operations Bureau
Commander Rogert F. DeSteunder
Secretary Naomi Stok—974-2270

Canine Coordination
Sgt. Burt Quick—565-3253

Traffic Coordination
Lt. Kenneth Culver— 974-2089

San Diego County Sheriff's Office
Sheriff, Jim Roache
Assistant Sheriff, Maudie Bobbitt
974-2270
9621 Ridgehaven Ct.
San Diego, CA 92123
974-2222/FAX 974-2304

Encinitas Station
175 North El Camino Real
Encinitas, CA 92024-2899
Caption Charles Wood - 966-3550
Secretary Rita Phillips - 966-3565

Lt. Dennis Cole - 966-3560
Operations Sergeant - 966-3542
Patrol Sergeant - 966-3548
Crime Prevention - 966-3583
Carol Cottingham - 966-3520
Traffic - 966-3511
Public - 753-1252
FAX 942-5093

Imperial Beach Station
845 Imperial Beach Boulevard
Imperial Beach, CA 91932-2796
Captain Joseph Cellucci - 498-2400
Secretary Elaine Cantrell - 498-2400
Lt. Florence Helms - 498-2400
Operations Sergeant - 498-2415
Patrol Sergeant - 498-2434
Public - 498-2400
FAX 575-6754

Lemon Grove Station
3240 Main Street
Lemon Grove, CA 91945-1705
Captain William Flores - 441-4042
Secretary Ginny Nazworth - 441-4043
Lt. Octavia Collins (Admin.) - 441-4044
Lt. Dave Herbert (Field) - 441-4045
Operations Sergeant - 441-4046
Patrol Sergeant - 441-4058
Crime Prevention, Karen Smith - 441-4037
Detectives - 441-4053
Juvenile Intervention - 441-4034
Traffic - 441-4029
Public - 441-4100
Victim/Witness Program:
  Marianne Gallagher - 441-4047
  Fran Noe - 441-4785
FAX 441-4020
Poway Station
12935 Pomerado Rd.
Poway, CA 92064-5325
Captain Yolanda Collins - 738-2532
Secretary Gabriella Fohr - 738-2532
Lt. Karen Axali - 738-2532

Operations Sergeant - 738-2511
Patrol - 738-2514
Crime Prevention, Becky King - 738-2506
Public (toll free for Poway) - 738-2532
(other users) 738-2532
FAX 748-7954

Santee Station
8511 Cuyamaca Street
Santee, CA 92071-4288
Captain Charles Lane - 258-3119
Secretary Marsi Brown - 258-3125
Lt. Kurt Fettu (Admin.) - 258-3120
Lt. Daniel Canfield (Field) - 258-3256
Operations Sergeant - 258-3076
Patrol Sergeant - 258-3077
Crime Prevention, Cyndi Forsythe - 258-3127
Detectives - 258-3101
Juvenile Intervention - 258-3106
Traffic - 258-3180
After Hours Only - 258-3078
Public - 258-3100
FAX 258-3096

Vista Station
325 South Melrose Dr., Suite 210
Vista, CA 92083-6627
Captain Dennis Kollar - 940-4559
Secretary Kyle Norman - 940-4559
Lt. Frank Nunez (Admin.) - 940-4560
Lt. Edward Lubic (Field) - 940-4566
Operations Sergeant - 940-4325
Patrol Sergeant - 940-4341
Crime Prevention, Nancy Aguilera - 940-4564
Detectives - 940-4571
Drug Education Unit - 940-4878
Juvenile Intervention - 940-4547
Squad Room - 940-4543
Street Narcotics Enforcement - 940-4561
Traffic - 940-4556
Public - 940-4551
FAX 630-9366

Alpine Substation
1247 Tavern Road
Alpine, CA 91901-3820
Lt. John Falconer - 579-4136
Secretary Bonnie Hileman - 579-4136
Inside - 579-4003
Public - 579-4136

Fallbrook Substation
127 East Hawthorne St.
Fallbrook, CA 92028-2052
Lt. Robert Takeshta - 723-6067
Secretary Connie McFarland - 723-6050
Inside - 723-6067
Public - 723-6050
Detectives 723-6060
FAX 731-6312

Bonsall Office
5256 South Mission Rd.
Bonsall, CA 92003-3620
Main/Public 724-0869

Ramona Substation
1424 Montecito Rd.
Ramona, CA 92065-5200
Lt. Gerald Finley - 738-2499
Secretary Dianna Ranes - 738-2499
Inside - 738-2499
Public - 789-1200
Public Business Office - 789-9157
FAX 788-9077

San Marcos Substation
187 Santar Place
San Marcos, CA 92069
Lt. Scott McClintock - 736-2140 x3020
Secretary Ann Kendall - 736-2140 x3012
Sergeant's Office - 736-2140 x3023
Squad Room - 736-2140 x3032
Detectives (menu select) - 736-2140
Public - 736-2140
FAX 736-2161

Valley Center/Pauma Substation
28205 North Lake Wohlford
Valley Center, CA 92082-8742
Lt. Doug Clements - 749-7318
Secretary Jan Zatlokowicz - 749-1309
Sgt. Donald Continelli - 749-7163
Inside - 749-1309
Public - 749-1303

RURAL LAW ENFORCEMENT DIVISIONS

Julian Substation
1485 Hollow Glen Road
P.O. Box 369
Julian, CA 92036-0369
Lt. George Kneeshaw - 765-0161
Secretary Roseanna Inouye - 765-0161
Inside - 765-0161
Public - 765-0503
Indian Reservation Enforcement Detail
Sgt. Kenny Prue - 765-0161
FAX 765-3285

Campo/Tecate Substation
378 Sheridan Road
P.O. Box 7
Campo, CA 91906-0007
Sgt. Walter Ogle - 440-1065
Secretary Marcella Guerrero - 440-1065
Inside - 440-1065
Public - 478-5378
FAX 478-9076

Pine Valley Substation
28848 Old Highway 80
P.O. Box 312
Pine Valley, CA 91962-0312
Sgt. Felix Bustamante - 445-3914
Secretary Barbara Rust - 445-3914
Inside - 440-1065
Public - 478-5378
FAX 478-9076

Borrego Springs Office
610 Palm Canyon Dr.
P.O. Box 323
Borrego Springs, CA 92004-0323
Inside/Public - 767-5656
Secretary Roseanna Inouye
(at Julian) - 765-0161

Boulevard/Jacumba Office
33919 Highway 94
P.O. Box 1117
Boulevard, CA 91905-0217
Inside/Public 766-4585
Secretary Barbara Rust
(at Pine Valley) - 473-8774

Dulzura Office
P.O. Box 306
Dulzura, CA 91917-0306
Inside/Public 468-3268
Secretary Marcella Guerrero (at Campo)
- 476-5378

Ranchita Warner Springs Office
25694 San Felipe Rd.
Warner Springs, CA 92088
Sgt. Doyle Krouskop - 782-4107
Secretary Roseanna Inouye
(at Julian) - 765-0161
Public - 782-3352
Inside - 782-4107
FAX 782-4106

CITY POLICE DEPARTMENTS

Carlsbad Police Dept.
2560 Orion Way
Carlsbad, CA 92008
931-2100

Chula Vista Police Dept.
276 4th Avenue
Chula Vista, CA 91910
691-5137

Coronado Police Dept.
578 Orange Avenue
Coronado, CA 92118
522-7350

El Cajon Police Dept.
100 Fletcher Parkway
El Cajon, CA 92020
579-3391

Escondido Police Dept.
700 W. Grand Ave.
Escondido, CA 92025
741-4721

La Mesa Police Dept.
8181 Allison Drive
La Mesa, CA 91931
469-6111

National City Police Dept.
1200 National City Blvd.
National City, CA 91950
336-4400

San Diego Police Department
1401 Broadway
San Diego, CA 92101
531-2000
Area Stations:
Central Division
1401 Broadway MS 748
San Diego, CA 92101
525-8400
Logan Heights, Downtown San Diego
Eastern Division
9225-Aero Drive
San Diego, CA 92123
495-7900
Hwy 805 to La Mesa/Miramar Rd.
to Hwy 94
Northern Division
4275 Eastgate Mall
San Diego, CA 92037
552-1700

*Clairemont, Pacific Beach, Mission
Beach, University City, South Del Mar,
Torey Pines Rd.*
Northeastern Division
13396 Salmon River Rd.
San Diego,, CA 92129
538-8000
*Rancho Penasquitos, Rancho Bernardo,
Scripps Ranch, Mira Mesa*
Southern Division
1120 27th Street
San Diego, CA 92154
690-8300
*South of Chula Vista, Pacific Ocean to
Otay Mesa*
Southeastern Division
7222 Skyline Drive
San Diego, CA 92114
527-3500
Southeast San Diego
Western Division
5215 Gaines Street
San Diego, CA 92110
692-4800
*North Park, Hillcrest, Ocean Beach,
Linda Vista, Old Town*

Oceanside Police Dept.
1617 Mission Ave.
Oceanside, CA 92054
966-4900

Social Security Administration Offices
Information (800)772-1213

Chula Vista
380 3rd. Ave. Suite B
Chula Vista, CA 91910

El Cajon
1068 Broadway, Second Floor
El Cajon, CA 92021

Escondido
205 W. Mission Ave., Suite G
Escondido, CA 92035

La Mesa
7373 University Avenue
La Mesa, CA 91941

Linda Vista
7691 Dagget St.
San Diego, CA 92111

National City
2530 E. Plaza Blvd.
National City, CA 91950

Oceanside
1305 Union Plaza Ct.
P.O. Box 1039
Oceanside, CA 92054

Pacific Beach
909 Girard Ave.
Pacific Beach, CA 92109
Downtown
880 Front Street, Suite 1265
San Diego, CA 92101

Hospital and Health Clinics

County of San Diego
Psychiatric Hospital
3851 Rosecrans St.
San Diego, CA 92110
Admissions 692-8200
Administration, billing 692-8232

Department of Veterans Affairs
Medical Center
3350 La Jolla Village Dr.
San Diego, CA 92161
General Information 552-8505
Medical Administration Management -

billing 552-8585 x3474
Admissions M-F 8am-4pm 552-7407
Admissions after hours 552-7523

Edgemoor Geriatric Hospital
9065 Edgemoor Dr.
Santee, CA 92071
258-3001

COUNTY HEALTH CLINICS

East San Diego Health Center
5202 University Ave.
San Diego, CA 92105
229-7990/ FAX 265-2459

El Cajon Public Health Center
113 E. Douglas Ave.
El Cajon, CA 92020
579-4446/ FAX 579-4068

Escondido Public Health Center
606 East Valley Parkway
Escondido, CA 92025
740-4000/ FAX 740-4003
North San Diego Health Center
2440 Grand Ave.
San Diego, CA 92109
581-4300/ FAX 581-4305

Oceanside Health Center
104 S. Barnes
Oceanside, CA 92054
967-4401/ FAX 967-4644

South Bay Public Health Center
500 Third Ave.
Chula Vista, CA 91910
691-4525/ FAX 691-4616

Unemployment—EDD

Disability Insurance Claims
P.O. Box 831

San Diego, CA 92112
Location (no mail):
5333 Mission Center Road
237-7586/ FAX 238-3600

Unemployment Insurance Claims
E.D.D.
1354 Front St.
San Diego, CA 92101
525-4522, 525-4248/ FAX 525-4830

E.D.D.
P.O. Box 15-C
El Cajon, CA 92022
Location (no mail)
1360 N. Magnolia Ave.
441-1373

E.D.D.
2027 E. Mission Ave.
Oceanside, CA 92054
757-1281/ FAX 439-6036

E.D.D.
1664 Industrial Blvd.
Chula Vista, CA 91915
575-0191/ FAX 575-7546

E.D.D.
4579 Mission Gorge Pl.
San Diego, CA 92120
265-4880/ FAX 265-4873

E.D.D.
6145 Imperial Ave.
San Diego, CA 92114
264-1616/ FAX 527-7821

San Diego Gas & Electric
General Information 239-7511
Billing questions can be handled by
calling the number printed at the bottom
of you billing statement

Clairemont District Office
4340 Genesee Ave., Suite 103
San Diego, CA 92117
495-8901/ FAX 495-8904

Downtown San Diego Branch Office
101Ash St.
San Diego, CA 92101
696-4070/ FAX 699-5098

Eastern District Office
104 N. Johnson Ave.
El Cajon, CA 92020
441-3805/ FAX 441-3936
Escondido District Office
1605 East Valley Parkway
Escondido, CA 92027
738-6700/ FAX 738-6722

Mission Valley District Office
2525 Camino del Rio South, Ste. 335
San Diego, CA 92108
497-1445/ FAX 497-1446

North Coast District Office
5875 Avenida Encinas
Carlsbad, CA 92088
438-6036/ FAX 438-7684

South Bay District Office
436 H Street
Chula Vista, CA 91910
482-3305/FAX 482-3349

BOARD OF PORT
COMMISSIONERS

Coronado
Raymond W. Burk, *Chairman*
Imperial Beach
Frank J. Urtasun, *Vice Chairman*
San Diego
Susan Lew, *Secretary*
Clifford W. Graves, *Commissioner*
J. Michael McDade, *Commissioner*

Chula Vista
Robert Penner, *Commissioner*
National City
Jess Van Deventer, *Commissioner*

Media

These are highlights of the media in San Diego. For a complete listing of print, television, radio and speciality media, subscribe to the Finder Binder by calling 463-5050.

Alpine Sun
P.O. Box 1089
Alpine, CA 91903-1089
445-3280 or 445-3288
Managing Editor - Jay Harn
Deadline - One week prior to publication

Beach & Bay Press
San Diego Community Newspaper
Group
P.O. Box 9550
San Diego, CA 92169-0550
270-3103/ FAX 270-9325
Editor -John Gregory

Blade-Citizen
P.O. Box 90
Oceanside, CA 92049
433-7333, 457-1970 toll-free
City Editor - Peg Sagen
Human Interest Columnist - Brian Cook

Coronado Journal
1224 10th St. Suite 102
Coronado, CA 92118-3419
435-3141/ FAX 435-3051
Editor - Kelly Pyrek

Daily Californian
P.O. Drawer 1565
El Cajon, CA 92022-1565
442-4044/ FAX 447-6165

Editor - Nancy Weingartner
Zone Editor - Laurie Arnold

La Jolla LIght
P.O. Box 1927
La Jolla, CA 92038
459-4201/ FAX 459-0977
Editor - Roderick Pressly
Political writer - Cindy Queen

The Reader
P.O. Box 85803
San Diego, CA 92186-5803
235-3000/ FAX 231-0489
Editor - Jim Holman
Deadline three days prior to publication

San Diego Business Journal
4909 Murphy Canyon Rd., Suite 200
San Diego, CA 92123-4300
277-6359/ FAX 277-2149
Editor - Martin Hill

San Diego Daily Transcript
P.O. Box 85469
San Diego, CA 92186-5469
232-4381/ FAX 236-8126
City Editor - Priscilla Lister

San Diego Home/Garden
P.O. Box 1471
San Diego, CA 92112-1471
233-4567/ FAX 233-1004
Editor - Dirk Sutro

San Diego Magazine
P.O. Box 85409
San Diego, CA 92138-5409
225-8953/ FAX 222-0773
Managing Editor - Winke Self
Deadline six weeks prior to publication

San Diego Union-Tribune
P.O. Box 191
San Diego, CA 92112-4106
299-3131/FAX 293-1896 city desk 293-

2148 newsroom
For direct calls, dial 293 plus extention:
Editor in Chief - Herb Klein - 1111
City Editor - Ray Kipp - 2235
Metro Editor - Carl Larsen - 2075
News Editor - Jim Ketchum - 1308
County Editor - Tom Nolan - 1205
Politics Editor - Margaret King - 1256
Columnist - Tom Blair - 1518
State Writer - Gordon Smith
Government Overview - Ray Huard
Legal Affairs Writer - Lorie Hearn
Features Consumer Writer - Bobbi
Ignelzi
Politics Writer - John Marelius
North County Coastal
820 S. Hill St.
Oceanside, CA 92054
722-1595
Oceanside Bureau - Ron Ham
North County Inland
220 W. 2nd Avenue
Escondido, CA 92025
(800) 244-6397
Escondido Bureau - John Cannon
East County
185 West Madison
El Cajon, CA 92020
593-4949
El Cajon Bureau - John Gilmore
South Bay
555 H. Street
Chula Vista, CA 92010
293-1754
Chula Vista Bureau - Irene Jackson

San Diego Voice & Viewpoint
1729 N. Euclid Ave.
San Diego, CA 92105-5414
266-2233/ FAX 266-0533
Editor - John Warren

Star-News (south)
P.O. Box 1207
Chula Vista, CA 91910-1207

427-3000/ FAX 426-6346
City Editor - Jamie Smith

Times-Advocate
207 E. Pennsylbania Ave.
Escondido, CA 92025-2888
745-6611/ FAX 745-3769
Editor - Richard Peterson
Editorial Editor - Logan Jenkins

RADIO—TALK FORMAT

KFMB
P.O. Box 85888
San Diego, CA 92186-5888
292-7600/ FAX 279-7676 (AM)
News Director - Cliff Albert

KSDO
5050 Murphy Canyon Rd.
San Diego, CA 92123-4399
278-1130/FAX 285-4364 newsroom
Exec. Talk Show Producer - Gayle
Falkenthal

**The Roger Hedgecock Show
phone lines**
San Diego - 560-1130
NC Inland - 745-1130
NC Coastal - 436-1130
South Bay/East County - 669-1130

TELEVISION

KFMB - Channel 8
P.O. Box 85888
San Diego, CA 92138-5888
571-8888/FAX 560-0627 newsroom
Assignment Editor - Rebecca Millman

KGTV - Channel 10
P.O. Box 85347
San Diego, CA 92186
237-1010 FAX 527-0369 newsroom
Assignment Editor - M-F Midday - Jack

Moorhead
M-F 11 p.m. - Brad McLellan
Weekends - Jack Weber

KNSD - Channel 39
8330 Engineer Road
San Diego, CA 92111-2493
279-3939, 279-1385 newsroom
FAX 492-9143 newsroom
News Director - Irv Kass

KPBS
5164 College Avenue
San Diego State University
San Diego, CA 92182-0527
594-1515/ FAX 265-6417
Program Production Director - Gloria
Penner

KUSI - Channel 51
4575 Viewridge Ave.
San Diego, CA 92123
571-5151/ FAX 576-9317
News Director - Paul Beavers

CABLE TELEVISION

American Cablevision of Coronado -
435-0157
General Manager - Michael Bauerfeind

Country Cable - 789-2663
Office Manager - Helen Baldwin

Cox Cable San Diego -
263-9251/ FAX 266-5540
General Manager - Robert McRann

Daniels Cablevision, Inc. -
438-7741/ FAX 438-8461
General Manager - Joni Odum

Jones Intercable of San Diego, Inc. -
660-0405/ FAX 670-7717
General Manager - Gary McDonald

Julian Cablevision - 765-1795
General Manager - Margaret McNichols
San Diego's Learning Channel (ITV) -
292-3742/ FAX 467-1549
Station Manager - Harry Weinberg

Southwestern Cable TV -
695-3110/ FAX 536-8203
Community Program Supervisor - Dan
Ballister

Telecable 767-5607/ FAX 767-3609
General Manager - Arthur Barnett

Times-Mirror Cable TV -
599-6060/ FAX 598-5601
General Manager - Thomas Tomkins

Valley Center Cable - 749-1402
General Manager - Jerry Schwartz

Courts

**Office of the Attorney General
San Diego**
110 West A Street, Ste. 700
San Diego, CA 92101
237-7351

U.S. District Court
U.S. Courthouse Building
940 Front Street
San Diego, CA 92189
Clerk's Office - 557-5600
U.S. Attorney
William Branniff - 557-5610
Chief Asst. U.S. Attorney
James W. Brannigan, Jr. - 557-6067
U.S. Marshal
Richard W. Cameron - 557-6620
Chief U.S. Probation Officer
Mark W. Fisher - 557-6650
U.S. District Court Clerk
Don Hendrix - 557-5600

Chief Judge
Hon. Judith N. Keep -557-5542
Hon. Rudi M. Brewster -557-6190
Senior Judge
Hon. William B. Enright, - 557-5537
Hon. Earl B. Gilliam - 557-6625
Hon. Marilyn L. Huff -557-6016
Senior Judge
Hon. Leland Nielsen - 557-5391
Hon. John S. Rhoades -557-5960
Senior Judge
Hon. Edward J. Schwartz -557-6262
Hon. Gordon Thompson, Jr.
557-6480
Senior Judge
Hon. Howard B. Turrentine-
557-6630
Hon. Irma E. Gonzalez -557-7107
U. S. Magistrates
Hon. Roger C. McKee - 557-5874
Hon. Harry R. McCue - 557-5585
Hon. Barry Ted Moskowitz - 557-5583
Hon. Louisa S. Porter
Hon. Leo S. Papas
U.S. Trustee
Southern District of California
101 W. Broadway, Ste. 440
SanDiego, CA 92101
557-5013/ FAX 557-5339
U.S. Trustee -
Sandra J. Wittman
Regional Asst. U.S. Trustee -
Larry G. Ramey
Asst. U.S. Trustee - John Patrik Boyl
Attorney - Tiffany L. Corroll
Attorney - David R. Musgrave
Attorney - Mary Testerman

Municipal Court of the San Diego Judicial District
220 West Broadway
San Diego, CA 02121
General Information - 239-6864
Presiding Judge -
H. Ronald Domnitz - 521-3019

Court Adminstrator -
D. Kent Pedersen - 531-3114
Marshal -
Michael Sgobba - 531-3995
Presiding Dept.
2013 Courthouse - 531-3107
Kimberly Youn, Clerk - 531-3019
Pat Barradas, Chief Judicial Secretary -
531-3056
Felony Arraignment Dept. 2016
Courthouse - 531-3020
Misdemeanor Arraignment Dept. 1008
Courthouse - 531-3021
Trial Setting Dept. 1007 Courthouse -
531-3022
Presiding Calendar 2014 Courthouse -
531-3105

Civil Building
1409 Fourth Ave.
San Diego, CA 92101
Civil Information - 687-2086
Tentative Rulings - 687-2190
Civil Proceedings Dept. C1 - 687-2001
Civil Dept. C2 - 687-2002
Civil Dept. C3 - 687-2003
Civil Dept. C4 - 687-2004
Judicial Secretary - 687-2090

Traffic Arraignment and Small Claims Court
8950 Clairemont Mesa Blvd.
San Diego, CA 92123
Traffic Information - 565-2234
Small Claims Information
687 - 2080
Judicial Secretary - 694-2151

Judges
Hon. E. Mac Amos, Jr.
Clerk - George Kuettner
Hon. Rafael A. Arreola
Clerk - John T. Belden
Hon. Jay M. Bloom
Clerk - Kelly A. Andrews

Hon. Frank A. Brown
Clerk - Susan Esqueda
Hon. Robert C. Coates
Clerk - Joan Cooper
Hon. Patricia A. Y. Cowette
Clerk - Marian L. Hall
Hon. David J. Danielsen
Clerk - Jeff Porch
Hon. Richard J. Hanscom
Clerk - Gary D. Urie
Hon. Judith F. Hayes
Clerk - Kathy Morton
Hon. Harvey Hiber
Clerk - Ann Rollings
Hon. Gale E. Kaneshiro
Clerk - Frieda McCurley-Gulley
Hon. Nicholas Kasimatis
Clerk - Vivian Hall
Hon. Janet I. Kintner
Clerk - Charles D. Spenser
Hon. Terry J. Knoepp
Clerk - Debra Roth
Hon. Lillian Y. Lim
Clerk - Annette Draper
Hon. Joe O. Littlejohn
Clerk - Wanda Miramontes
Hon. Robert P. McDonald
Clerk - Ann McCall
Hon. Michael B. Orfield
Clerk - Jacqueline L Feaster
Hon. Charles L. Patrick
Clerk - Robin Bariring
Hon. Charles G. Rogers
Clerk - Trudy Marshall
Hon. Howard H. Shore
Clerk - Linda Jackson
Hon. Lawrence W. Stirling
Clerk - Patricia Seavey
Hon. Timothy W. Tower
Clerk - Michelle Eston-Pike
Hon. Joan P. Weber
Clerk - Teresa Dusi
Hon. Ann P. Winebrenner
Clerk - Lynn Rockwell
Hon. William H. Woodward

Clerk - Lori Gleason Urie
Commissioners
Hon. James L. Duchnick
Hon. Carol Mushing Frausto
Hon. Michael S. Goodman
Hon. Jerome E. Varon
Hon. Duncan S. Werth, II
Hon. James A. Wilson
Hon. Lee C. Witham

Municipal Court of the North County Judicial District
325 S. Melrose Dr., Ste. 120
Vista, CA 92083-6693
Court Administrator
Patricia M. Johns,
Asst. Court Administrator
Sharon A. Lear
Court Administrator - 940-4633
Criminal Records - 940-4644
Attorney Services - 940-4621
Civil - 740-4021
Judicial Secretary - 940-4728

Court Reporters
Bea Tannen - 940-4715
Michael Provinse - 940-4717
Elaine Cohen - 940-4717
Glenda Backman - 940-4580

**Escondido Branch -
Civil, Small Claims**
800 E. Valley Parkway
Escondido, CA 92025-3098
Civil - 740-4021
Small Claims - 740-4045

San Marcos Branch - Minor Offense
338 Via Vera Cruz
San Marcos, CA 92069-2693
Attorney Services - 940-2806
Presiding Judge
Hon. Harley J. Karwicker
Clerk - Donna Stagliano
Hon. Michael L. Burley

172

Clerk - Virginia Williams
Hon. William B. Draper, Jr.
Clerk - Carmen Wagner
Hon. Harry Elias
Clerk - Karon Callahan
Hon. Michael B. Harris
Clerk - Leticia Almaraz
Hon. Susanne W. Knquf
Clerk - Melissa Shoop
Hon. Luther L. Leeger
Clerk - Kay Storm
Hon. Victor E. Ramirez
Clerk - Jessica Bermis
Hon. Donald E. Rudloff
Clerk - Kathleen Crooks
Hon. David W. Ryan
Clerk - Martha Larsen
Hon. Marguerite L. Wagner
Clerk - Pam Fiscus

Commissioners
Hon. Anthony J. Brandenburg
Hon. Daniel Ornelas
Hon. Larry Jones

Municipal Court of the South Bay Judicial District
500 C Third Ave.
Chula Vista, CA 91910
Court Administrator
Stephen W. Thunberg,
Court Secretary - 691-4770
Criminal/Traffic - 691-4628
Calendar - 691-4738
Civil - 691-4639
Small Claims - 691-4439
Bail Unit - 691-4754
Accounting - 691-4775
Dept. One - vacant
Dept. Two
Hon. Susan Finlay
Clerk - Marilyn Ryan
Dept. Three
Hon. Karen Ryman
Clerk - Irene Kimbrough

Traffic Referee/Commission
Dept. Four
Hon. Ernest Bonuda
Clerk - Lynn Babers
Dept. Five
Hon. William S. Cannon
Clerk - Rose Brown
Dept. Six
Hon. Terry Scott
Clerk - Armida Barron-Espinosa
Dept. Seven - vacant
Dept. Eight
Hon. Roy B. Cazares
Clerk - Michele Peters
Dept. Ten
Hon. Dianne K. O'Connor
Clerk - Norma Olvera

Court Reporters
William J. Barton, CSR - 691-4443
Dollie D. Wilson, CSR - 691-4768

Municipal Court of the El Cajon Judicial District
250 E. Main STreet
El Cajon, CA 92020
Court Administrator
Frederick W. Lear
Asst. Court Administrator
Michelle S. Longlin
Judicial Secretary - 441-4475
Administrative Secretary - 441-4336
Calendar - 441-4481
Civil - 441-4461
Courtroom Clerks - 441-4342
Criminal - 441-4342
Small Claims - 441-4276
Accounting - 441-4486
Traffic/Minor Offenses - 441-4274

Ramona Branch
1428 Montecito Rd.
Ramona, CA 92065
441-4244, 738-2400
Presiding Judge

173

Hon. William Mcgrath
Asst. Presiding Judge
Hon. Patricia K. Cookson
Hon. Larrie R. Brainard
Hon. Elizabeth A. Riggs
Hon. Victor E. Bianchini
Hon. Susan D. Huguenor
Hon. Eddie C. Sturgeon
Hon. Christine K. Goldsmith
Hon. Lantz Lewis
Commissioner R. Craig Woll
Traffic Referee/Commissioner Robert W. Rankin

Court Reporters
Bonita Madden - 441-4308
Dale Cunningham - 441-4307
Lori Mosso - 441-4310

San Diego County Superior Court
220 West Broadway
San Diego, CA 92101
Executive Officer and Clerk - Kenneth E. Martone - 531-3820
Asst. Executive Officers
Michael Roddy - 531-3870
Pat Sweeten - 531-3820
Business Office - 531-3141
Arbitration - 531-3818
Grand Jury - 236-2675
Court Reporters - 531-3964
Calendar - 531-3960
Tentative Rulings - 531-3690 a.m., 531-3691 p.m.
Records - 531-3151
Pro-Tem Settlement Conferences - 531-3240

North County Branch
325 S. Melrose Dr.
Vista, CA 92083
Business Office - 940-4442

El Cajon Branch
250 East Main STreet

El Cajon, CA 92020
Business & Records - 441-4622

South Bay Branch
500 C Third Avenue
Chula Vista, CA 91910
Court Services - 691-4754

Juvenile Division
2851 Meadowlark Drive
San Diego, CA 92123
General Infomration - 694-4535

Family Court
1551-55 Sixth Avenue
San Diego, CA 92101
Business Office - 557-2030
Presiding Judge
Hon. Aurthor W. Jones
Clerk - Patricia Burke-Jennings
531-3795
Asst. Presiding Judge
Hon. James R. Miliken
Clerk - Crystal Lunt
531-3590
Hon G. Dennis Adams
Clerk - Phyllis Corzine
Hon. Thomas Ashword, III
Clerk - Lilia Garibay-Sanchez
Hon. Robert Baxley
Hon. Michael Bollman
Clerk - Al Lum
Hon. Federico Castro
Clerk - Debbie Tierman
Hon. Vincent P. Di Figlia
Clerk - Mary Rademaker
Hon. Raymond Edwards, Jr.
Clerk - Charlene Wright
Hon. Norbert Ehrenfreund
Clerk - Colleen Lewis
Hon. Herbert J. Exarhos
Clerk - Kathleen Koman
Hon. Barbara T. Gamer
Clerk - Carol Bozlee
Hon. David M. Gill

Clerk - Kristie Bircumshaw
Hon. Michael I. Greer
Clerk - Phyllis Bernstein
Hon. Lisa Guy-Schall
Clerk - Marilyn Peabody
Hon. Richard Haden
Clerk - Sandy Tabachki
Hon. Judith L. Haller
Clerk - Julie Watkins
Hon. Laura P. Hammes
Clerk - Holly Saenz
Hon. Charles R. Hayes
Clerk - Brenda Tom
Hon. Herbert B. Hoffman
Clerk - Rosemarie Sims
Hon. Harrison R. Hollywood
Clerk - Marilyn Golisch
Hon. William J. Howatt, Jr.
Clerk - Karen Kennard
Hon. Ronald L Johnson
Clerk - Paula Frank
Hon. Napoleon A. Jones, Jr.
Clerk - Naomi Stephens
Hon. Anthony C. Joseph
Clerk - Mary Ann Mases
Hon. Lawrence Kapiloff
Clerk - Marilou Alcantar
Hon. William H. Kennedy
Clerk - Ernest Marshall
Hon. Elizabeth Z. Kutzner
Clerk - Z.R. Gutierrez
Hon. J. Perry Langford
Clerk - Sylvia Kirchman
Hon. Melinda J. Lasater
Clerk - Tipin Johnson
Hon. Thomas O. LaVoy
Clerk - Rosemarie Sandoval
Hon. Morgan Lester
Clerk - Sharon Hicks
Hon. Frederic L. Link
Clerk - Silvia Houseman
Hon. Runston Maine
Clerk - Patti Roman
Hon. James A. Malkus
Clerk - Bonnis Rundle

Hon. Wesley R. Mason, III
Clerk - Helen Pfister
Hon. Robert E. May
Clerk - Claire Shea
Hon. Judith McConnell
Clerk - Jean Peterson
Hon. Donald L. Meloche
Clerk - Marie Ervin
Hon. Kevin Midlam
Clerk - Cathy Brown
Hon. Milton Milkes
Clerk - Joanne McLean
Hon. Jeffrey T. Miller
Clerk - Rose Nappi
Hon. Franklin J. Mitchell,Jr.
Clerk - Sharon Kush
Hon. Thomas R. Mitchell
Hon. Alpha L. Montgomery
Clerk - Carmen Gutierrez
Hon. David B. Moon, Jr.
Clerk - Delrene Sims
Hon. William D. Mudd
Clerk - Peggy Sirna
Hon. Richard M. Murphy
Clerk - Sandy Seematter
Hon. Robert J. O'Neill
Clerk - Toni Neumann
Hon. Terry B. O'Rourke
Clerk - Maureen Farias
Hon. Christine B. Pate
Clerk - Shakti Rose
Hon. William C. Pate
Clerk - Jane Heins
Hon. Wayne L. Peterson
Clerk - Laura Nicks
Hon. Ronald S. Prager
Clerk - Joanne Poynter
Hon. Allan J. Preckel
Clerk - Linda Rolan
Hon. Linda B. Quinn
Clerk - Mary Jean Barham
Hon. Seridan E. Reed
Clerk - Judy Dara
Hon. Bernard E. Revak
Clerk - Linda Savitz

Hon. Peter E. Riddle
Clerk - Carmen Walker
Hon. Jesus Rodriguez
Clerk - Carolyn Burgess
Hon. Philip Sharp
Clerk - Teresa Ganelin
Hon. Robert C. Thaxton, Jr.
Clerk - Nellie Pernicano
Hon. John M. Thompson
Clerk - Sherry Blevins
Hon. Daniel J. Tobin
Clerk - Douglas CArlson
Hon. Michael Wellington
Clerk - Douglas Peck
Hon. Thomas J. Whelan
Clerk - Jerri Barnes
Hon. S. Charles Wickersham
Clerk - Mary Kaneyuki
Hon. Raymond F. Zvetina
Clerk - Rena Henry

Referees
Hideo Chino
Clerk - Juanita Lessa
Bonnie M. Dumanis
Clerk - Karla Larson
Yuri Hofmann
Clerk - Diane Hartje
Michael J. Imhoff
Clerk - Kathy Mormile

Commissioners
Alan B. Clements
Clerk - Jennifer Pecore
Etta Gillivan
Clerk - Mary Holbrook

Court of Appeal, Fourth Appellate District
Division One
750 B Street, Suite 500
San Diego, CA 92101
Stephen M. Kelly, Clerk - 237-7271
Gale Miller, Chief Deputy Clerk
Presiding Judge

Hon. Daniel J. Kremer - 237-7271
Hon. Howard B. Wiener - 237-7258
Hon. Don R. Work - 237-7748
Hon. William L Todd, Jr. - 237-7265
Hon. Patricia D. Benke - 237-7268
Hon. Richard D. Huffman - 237-7263
Hon. Charles W. Froehlich, Jr. - 238-3251
Hon. Gilbert Nares - 237-6096

U.S. Court of Appeals
U.S. Courthouse
940 Front Street
San Diego, CA 92189
Hon. J. Clifford Wallace,
Chief Judge 557-6114
Gevena P. LePre,
Administrative Assistant
Hon. David R. Thompson - 557-6400
Joan Westmoreland, Secretary

City Attorney's Office
City Administration Building
202 C Street, MS/3A
San Diego, CA 92101
236-6220

Civil Division
202 C Street, Third Floor
236-6220
John Witt, City Attorney
John M. Kaheny, Asst. City Attorney
Curtis M. Fitzpatrick, Asst. City
Attorney (Special Projects)
Janis Sammartino, Senior Chief Deputy
Stuart H. Swett, Senior Chief Deputy

Criminal Division
1200 Third AVe., Ste. 700
San Diego, CA 92101-4106
533-5500
Senior Chief Deputy
Susan M. Heath
Asst. Chief Deputy
David C. James

Litigation Division
1200 Third Ave., Ste. 1200'
San Diego, CA 92101 - 4106
533-5800
Eugene P. Gordon, Chief Deputy
C. Alan Sumption, Jr., Chief Deputy

**Office of the District Attorney,
County of San Diego**
District Attorney
Edwin L. Miller, Jr.,
Asst. District Attorney
Richard J. Neely,
Chief Deputy District Attorney
Brian E. Michaels,
San Diego—531-4040
220 W. Broadway
San Diego, CA 92101
San Diego—531-3544
101 W. Broadway, Ste. 1440
San Diego, CA 92101
San Diego—531-4070
101 W. Broadway, Ste. 700
San Diego, CA 92101
San Diego—531-4300
101 W. Broadway, Ste. 800
San Diego, CA 92101
Juvenile—694-4250
2851 Meadowlark Dr.
San Diego, CA 92123
East County—441-4588
250 E. Main St. 5th floor
El Cajon, CA 92020
North County—940-4301
325 S. Melrose Dr., Ste. 130
Vista, CA 92083
North County—940-6466
]410 S. Melrose Dr., Ste. 200
Vista, CA 92083
South Bay—691-4695
500 Third Avenue
Chula Vista, CA 91910

Below is the contact information for the people and/or groups whose stories appear in this book:

CHAPTER TWO
P.A.R.K.
Peoples Actions Rescuing Kids
Jim Tapscott - (619) 278-4114

CHAPTER FOUR
Light Up the Border
Muriel Watson - (619) 479-1125

CHAPTER FIVE
Jacarandas for San Diego
Donna Derrick - (619) 273-2489

Citizens Against Grafitti
Rosie Bystrak - (619) 427-3535

Silent No More
Cherie Chandler
3010 5th Ave. #202
San Diego, CA 92103
(619) 299-4233

CHAPTER ELEVEN
Citizen's Rule Book Committee
Jim Harnsburger - (619) 466-4920

United Taxpayers (UN-TAX)
Dick Rider
3161 Fryden Ct.
San Diego, CA 92117
(619) 273-1776

Dale Akiki Support Group
Rose Marie Royster - FAX (619) 673-2277